Marriage 101

As for God, His Way Is Perfect (Psalm 18:30 AB)

By

Jewell R. Powell

Casine

Thanks for your
support. Bless you

Jewell
Powell

This book is a work of fiction. Places, events, and situations in this story are purely fictional. Any resemblance to actual persons, living or dead, is coincidental.

ISBN: 0-9745528-0-1

This book is printed on acid free paper.

Unless otherwise indicated, all Scripture quotations are taken from the King James Version (KJV) of the Bible.

If you have testimonies or comments on any material in this book, please email me from the Rhema Books Web site at www.rhemabooks.com.

If you would like information pertaining to the ministry that has changed my life, or if you are interested in becoming a partner of that powerful ministry that will change *your* life, please write:

Victory Christian Ministry International
P.O. Box 441107
Fort Washington, MD 20749-1107

Acknowledgments

I would like to thank God for the gift of the Holy Spirit and the anointing through Jesus Christ that inspired me to write this book. Praise be to God!

I would like to thank my mighty man of valor, Lewis, for encouraging me to be all God has called me to be. Thanks to Lauren and Diamond, who probably don't even realize the sacrifices they made so that I could accomplish this project. I love you, and I thank God for blessing me with you three wonderful gifts.

I also would like to thank the following people: My parents, Della and Johnnie Jones. I thank God for you and what you have done and taught me over the years. I love you both very much. Also, my parents Almon and Ann Wheeler. I love you and I thank you for your love and support. To my sisters and brothers, Tuffie, Carla, Al, Lowell, April, Michael, Antionnette, Shanea, Elvin, and Shonté, whom I love dearly. Thank you so very much for believing in me and supporting me. To Crystal Simmons, thank you for your encouragement and for letting me bounce the ideas God has given me off of you. To Robin Dessau, thanks for being a cousin, proofreader, and best friend. Thanks to my loved ones, who have stuck by me through thick and thin: Kim Best, Danielle Finney, Patrice Pullen, Kim Shepherd, Lawanne Stewart, and Leslie Taylor. To my editors and to all those who prayed for me, thank you.

To my spiritual dad and mom, Pastors Tony and Cynthia Brazelton, whom I love dearly. Thank you for your passion and impartation of God's Word into my life so that I may live and prosper according to it.

Dedication

This book is dedicated to all those who are contemplating marriage as well as those who need to turn and take up their journey toward a heavenly marriage here on earth. Before we start this journey, I want us all to start off on the same page. For those who haven't given their lives to Jesus or who need to rededicate their faith, let us pray:

Father, I come before You as a sinner, and I thank You for sending Your only begotten Son for my sake. I know that Jesus died on the cross for my sins. I now acknowledge Jesus as Lord of my life. I know that I don't have to live by the world's standards because You have given me all that I need to live my life to the fullest through Your Word. I thank You that, right now, I am a new creature in Christ—I am no longer who I used to be. As I read this Word from You, my mind is open and my heart is prepared to be changed. Thank You, in Jesus' name. Amen.

Table of Contents

In the Midst

Each individual, completely separate, with all their
imperfections,
Takes a vow to become as one, but never realize their
connection.

Each promised to love, honor, and obey,
Then trials and tribulations came, and they forgot to
pray.

They never became one, so they are now still two,
Fighting like cats and dogs, they are so blue.

Be angry and sin not—nor let the sun go down upon
your wrath
That the Word would be a lamp unto your feet and a
light unto your path.

And why call me "Lord, Lord" and do not do the
things I say?
Whosoever comes to me and does as I say, will find
their way.

Can two walk together, except they be agreed?
Turn and take up your journey, for I am with thee.

A death must take place in order to bring life;
Put yourself upon the cross and present your bodies a
living sacrifice.

It's not difficult to do that, you see,
For Jesus has already paved the way for you and me.

For God is a God of order and decency—
Let it be in your heart, 1 Corinthians 11:3.

A marriage is a ministry in which people will see
That greater is He that lives on the inside of me.

So in order to live, you must die,
That your Heavenly Father herein be glorified.

There will be no marriages in the resurrection,
So let us be as angels here on earth before we go to
heaven.

—Jewell Powell

Foreword

I am sure that the process of writing a book must be much like giving birth to a child (neither of which have I attempted). However, I saw my wife go through the labor and delivery of our first biological child and the labor and delivery of writing and publishing her first book. Although the birthing process of our child was more of a physical challenge for my wife, I probably wouldn't venture far if I said both experiences were very challenging. If a man ever witnesses the child-bearing process, he never loses respect for the power God gave women! The same truth resides with me as I reflect on the many hours, days, weeks, and months of pure labor that my wife endured to give birth to her very first book, with many more to come. Her experience blessed and encouraged me as I witnessed the birthing process of this project, appropriately called *Marriage 101*. I love you and thank God for you, Honey!

When my wife asked me to write the foreword to her first book, I was honored. I'm honored because she wants me to set the stage for which you, the reader, will understand the importance of knowing God's plan and purpose for marriage, which is covered and easily understood in this book. I am also honored because I know that numerous marriages will be changed by what is written here. Thinking back before we got married, I can remember people saying, "There aren't any good books that will instruct couples in how to have a successful marriage." At the time I heard this statement, I never imagined that the mistakes that my wife and I would ultimately make would be the storyline of a how-to book that instructs couples. I can now say that there is a good book out there that will instruct couples in how to have a successful marriage.

This book will bless both men and women. It will change your thinking about the roles we (both men and women) play in the marriage covenant in today's society. It is anecdotal because it lends real life examples of how two individuals (Jewel and I) have strived for a better marriage relationship by overcoming real obstacles by gaining a clear understanding of what God says about marriage. We continue to have a successful marriage by implementing the Word of God daily in our lives. Most of all, *Marriage 101* will show you how to rebuild a marriage foundation that has been broken. In the book of Luke, Jesus instructs us, "Whosoever cometh to me, and heareth My sayings, and doeth them, I will show you to whom he is like: He is like a man which built an house, and digged deep, and laid the foundation on a rock: and when the flood arose, the streams beat vehemently upon that house, and it could not shake it: for it was founded upon a rock" (Luke 6:47-48). Because Jewel and I have rebuilt our marriage on the Word of God, it cannot be destroyed when the storms of life arise. We can testify today that, yes, marriage is and can be as wonderful and heavenly as God intended it to be.

I pray that the Rhema Word of God that has been brought forth in this book will bless you and your marriage.

— Lewis C. Powell

Introduction

After Lewis and I got married, he asked me, "Why are you doing things differently now? Before we got married, you cooked for me every day. . . you found me exciting. What changed?" Clowning around, I answered, "Mama taught me Marriage 101: Do what you need to do to get him (cook every day, make love frequently, etc.), and once the shackles are on, you don't have to do those things anymore." (My mother did not actually say this—I was joking.) I was always taught to have my own bank account in case the marriage didn't work out. I was also taught to work hard, always take care of myself, not depend on a man for anything, and be my own person.

In February 2001, I was in a dark place in my life. Lewis and I had just separated, and all I knew was that I loved my husband, but our marriage was not working. I began to wonder about God's purposes in creating the institution of marriage. Why would He create a union in which a man and a woman could not get along? Why would He want us to stay with an individual until death do us part, yet have us be so miserable and at odds all the time?

As I cried to the Lord to help me find the answers, the Holy Spirit told me that I didn't understand marriage because I was doing it *my* way. And later, after Lewis moved back home, the Holy Spirit told me to write all that God revealed to me about the way He intended marriage to be. When I asked what to name the book, He said, "This is Marriage 101 (let's go back to the basics and do it My way) What you thought and had been taught about marriage were wrong and out of order."

If you are going through hard times in your marriage right now, there is hope. There is nothing wrong with the institution; actually, it's very good if you do it God's way. The problem is with us, because we don't understand why He created marriage or even how it works. God created the covenant of marriage. So we need to let go of preconceived ideas we've learned from the world: television, movies, books, and the ideas and goals we had when we were growing up. Whenever we make a purchase (computer, stove, car, toaster, camera, etc.), we get instructions—a manual—and/or a customer service number to help us understand how to use it. Yet when it comes to marriage, God's institution, we don't go to His Word but to magazines, books, psychic hotlines, and so on. However, the Bible is supposed to be our manual.

I know that most of us have heard what the acronym BIBLE stands for: Basic Information Before Leaving Earth. The Bible is our instruction manual. It gives us everything we need to make it in life, especially in our marriages. God says His people perish because of the lack of knowledge (Proverbs 29:18). Marriages are destroyed because people lack the knowledge of what God says in His Word concerning them. Why would God create an institution that couldn't possibly work? He didn't. It's not the marriage covenant that is the problem; it's those who don't seek Him and get their wisdom, knowledge, and understanding from His Word.

For everyone who reads this book, my prayer is that the Word of God will jump off the pages into your life and change you. The purpose of this book is to lay a foundation. As you read it, God will give you answers (by the leading of the Holy Spirit) concerning your marriage, just as He did for me. If you will change your thinking and incorporate the truth that God will show you, your marriage *will* turn around, just as mine did. It took only two months for my marriage to improve because I did everything God told me to do. You have to purpose in your heart to submit to the Lord and to do all that He tells you to do. Is my marriage perfect today? No, but it is so much better, and with each passing day, it gets even better.

God wants believers to see that marriages are supposed to be patterned after Christ's love for the church. For example, Jesus (1) was born with a purpose, (2) was baptized, (3) was tempted by the devil, (4) began His ministry of truth and healing, (5) was crucified on the cross, (6) was resurrected from the dead, and (7) reconciled us back to God. As Peter reminds us, "To this you were called, because Christ suffered for you, leaving you an example, that you should follow in his steps" (1 Peter 2:21 NIV).

As I was formatting the chapters of this book, God gave me a humorous idea for structuring them. He suggested structuring them according to the Sleeping Beauty story. The story of Sleeping Beauty is a parable of Christ's love for the church and God's plan for marriage.

Now, let us take our journey to make our marriages all that God has called them to be.

All scripture is given by inspiration of God, and is profitable for doctrine, for reproof, for correction, for instruction in righteousness: That the man (and woman) of God may be perfect, thoroughly furnished unto all good works. (2 Timothy 3:16-17)

Parable of His Love

As you know, marriage is symbolic of the church per Ephesians 5:21-33. It shows how our marriages should reflect Jesus' love for the church. Christ is called the Bridegroom, and His church is called the bride. Throughout this book, each chapter will mention a part of the Sleeping Beauty story, yet it will give you an example to follow—Jesus.

As I was writing *Marriage 101*, I was led to revisit the story of Sleeping Beauty. After reading the story again, the Lord showed me that this fairytale is a parable of Christ's love for the church. Jesus taught in many parables throughout His ministry; and even today, we are able to continue receiving revelation from them. What is a parable? A parable is an earthly story with a heavenly meaning. The story of Sleeping Beauty has a valuable hidden meaning that can be revealed to you if you allow the Holy Spirit to show you. Once revealed, you will see the timeless story of God's eternal love for mankind and the sacrifice His Son Jesus Christ made over two thousand years ago by willfully dying on the cross to save mankind from their sins.

Before we begin our journey, allow me to set the stage for you and share the revelation the Lord revealed to me about this Walt Disney classic. Although the story is about a princess (the bride) who falls in love with the prince (bridegroom), the underlying story is how the prince sacrificed his life for her and what that sacrifice accomplished.

Sleeping Beauty represents the church—she is the bride. The prince represents the Bridegroom—Jesus. The title "Sleeping," which results from the curse that is put upon the princess, represents darkness. Darkness is symbolic of man's sin, rebellion, and ignorance. In John 12:35, Jesus says that he who walks about in the dark does not know where he goes; he is drifting. The evil fairy represents Satan, and her ugly creatures represent demons. As we know, light represents truth, goodness, and the Kingdom of God.

The fact that Sleeping Beauty is raised as a peasant girl is also symbolic. Every time Sleeping Beauty is mentioned as a peasant girl, God reminded me of the gift of salvation that was given to the Gentile nation through the redemptive blood of Jesus Christ. Although the Jews were God's chosen people under the old covenant, anyone who accepts His dear Son, Jesus Christ, under the new covenant has been adopted into His royal family. God instructs us in His Word, "But ye are a chosen generation, a royal priesthood, an holy nation, a peculiar people; that ye should show forth the praises of him who hath called you out of darkness into his marvelous light: Which in time past were not a people, but are now the people of God: which had not obtained mercy, but now have obtained mercy" (1 Peter 2:9-10).

The two kingdoms in the story represent two nations, the Jews (the prince kingdom) and the Gentiles (the bride's kingdom), which are now united as one because of the noble actions of the prince. Under the new covenant, there is neither Jew nor Greek (Gentile) but one body under the leadership of the Lord Jesus Christ (Galatians 3:28). The three fairies represent the Holy Trinity (Father, Son, and Holy Spirit).

For those who might not be familiar with the Sleeping Beauty story, here it is in a nutshell:

The Story of Sleeping Beauty

Once upon a time, there was a king and queen who celebrated the long-awaited birth of their daughter. It was a joyful day, and a feast was thrown throughout all the land to pay honor to her. All the people throughout the city brought gifts. Another king presented his son, and both monarchs prayed that their kingdoms would one day unite through the marriage of their children. In honor of the baby princess, three good fairies descended from the sky to give three special gifts. The first gave the gift of beauty and the second gave the gift of song. But before the third could give her gift, the evil fairy appeared in a blaze of fire. She was upset that no one had invited her to the special celebration. In her anger, she cursed the baby, saying that before she turned sixteen, she would die by pricking her finger on a spinning wheel.

God showed me that, just like the evil fairy put the curse on Sleeping Beauty's life, a curse was put on mankind. When the serpent deceived Eve, and she and Adam ate from the forbidden tree (Genesis 2:17), mankind was no longer under the Kingdom of God (light) but under Satan's authority (darkness).

Needless to say, the king and queen were quite upset. To comfort them, the good fairies reminded them that the third fairy had not yet given her gift. At this point, I saw the Holy Spirit giving comfort just as Jesus said He would do: "And I will pray the Father, and he shall give you another Comforter, that he may abide with you for ever" (John 14:16). The Greek word for comforter is *parakletos*, which literally means "one called alongside to help or an advocate." The Holy Spirit is called "another" comforter because in 1 John 2:1, it states that Jesus Himself is our advocate.

The king and queen exclaimed, "Can you reverse the curse?"

"No," the good fairy replied, "but I can change it somewhat. Instead of dying, she will sleep until true love kisses. Then she will awake."

No one—not the king nor the good fairies—could reverse the curse. Only true love could revoke it. In an effort to save his daughter from pricking her finger, the king made a decree throughout the city that all spinning wheels should be burned. The townspeople brought their spinning wheels and threw them into a bonfire.

In the meantime, the good fairies tried to find a way to do something to harm the evil fairy. However, realized they could only do good; there was no evil in them. So how could they stop the evil one from hurting Sleeping Beauty? One of the good fairies received revelation on how to stop the evil one. The one thing they knew about the evil fairy was that she didn't have what they had—love. The evil one didn't know or understand love or any other characteristic that makes up God's love.

My Bible defines all the fruits of the Spirit, as stated in Galatians 5:22-23, as follows: *Love* is the willing, sacrificial giving of oneself for the benefit of another without thought of return. *Joy* is gladness of heart. *Peace* is tranquility of mind, freeing oneself from worry or fear. *Long-suffering* is patience with others. It is the opposite of short temper, a disposition quietly bearing injury. *Gentleness* is kindness. *Goodness* is generosity. *Faith*, as to the fruit, means dependability. *Meekness* is humility, being teachable, thinking of others before your own needs. *Temperance* is self-control, the ability to control your desires. These are the characteristics we need to beat Satan at his deceitful tactics. We, as born-again believers, must overcome evil with good! The very nature of God is love. If we respond to the evil one with God's love, then Satan is paralyzed and will not be able to retaliate because we have just stopped him in his tracks. This is how we can keep the devil out our marriages, out of our homes, and out of our lives—by walking in God's character.

In a vain attempt to protect their daughter, the king and queen decided to keep the child hidden and safe until past her sixteenth birthday As part of their plan, the good fairies decided to live as mortals during those years to raise the princess in a hideaway place. Wow! In a loose analogy (since Jesus is divine), Jesus, too, had to live as a human here on the earth to accomplish God's perfect plan to save mankind from their sins. While in hiding, Sleeping Beauty had to live as a peasant girl, which was beneath her birthright. How many born-again believers who have given their lives to Christ (which means they are now adopted as children of God) are still living as peasants? Remember, God's Word says that we are a chosen generation, a royal priesthood.

There were many sad and lonely years for the king and his people as their beautiful princess remained hidden. Just like Sleeping Beauty, mankind was under a curse, sad and lonely for years because of the sin committed by Adam and Eve. We were in darkness and no longer had a direct relationship with God. Why? Because Adam and Eve's sin was disobedience, and sin separates us from God. During those hidden years, Sleeping Beauty continued to grow and mature into a beautiful young woman. Although Sleeping Beauty appeared on the outside as if she had everything, she was lonely. She was not living in the fullness of who she was as a princess, and she had not yet met her true prince. Just like Sleeping Beauty, when a person has not yet met or developed a relationship with the Prince of Peace, Jesus Christ, although their lives may appear on the outside to have everything, they are not living in the fullness of who God has called them to be.

Then, the princess met a man, whom she did not know was a prince, and they fell in love. The prince rushed to tell his father how he fell in love with a peasant girl. But his father, the king, was very upset with the news. A peasant girl? After reading how excited the prince was about falling in love, my first thought was the scripture in 1 John 4:19, "We love him, because He first loved us." The prince was so excited that he didn't care about who she was or where she came from. Our Prince, Jesus, feels the same way about us when we receive His love and accept Him as Lord and Savior of our lives. He doesn't care who we are, what we've done in the past, or what sins we are committing. He just loves us and receives us as we are. That is what is so awesome about the good news of Jesus Christ.

Like the prince, Sleeping Beauty ran home to tell the good news that she had fallen in love. To her surprise, she was told of her identity—that she was a princess, not a peasant—and was taken to meet her family. Before she could see her parents, the evil fairy put her in a trance, and she followed a spirit until she came to a spinning wheel. A voice said, "touch it," and Sleeping Beauty pricked her finger—just as the evil fairy had said she would—and fell into a deep sleep. The image of Sleeping Beauty being lured into a curse by a spirit was an awakening moment for me. I realized that the voice of the evil fairy was the same evil voice that told Eve to eat from the tree of good and evil. It is also the same voice that tells you and me to do something that is contrary to what God is telling us to do.

The good fairies didn't know how to tell Sleeping Beauty's father the terrible news. Instead, they put the whole kingdom to sleep. One act—a finger pricked on a spinning wheel—put the whole kingdom to sleep (think about it). However, before the kings were put to sleep, the prince's father tried to tell the other king that their kingdoms would not unite because the prince had fallen in love with a peasant girl. One of the good fairies overheard it, and immediately she knew that the prince was Sleeping Beauty's true love.

To thicken the plot, when the fairies arrived at the cottage where the prince was, they found that the evil fairy had already taken him. Now, they would have to go to the forbidden mountain to help the prince. At that time, the evil fairy, along with her ugly creatures, were celebrating with fire and laughter. They were teasing the prince, who was in the dungeon in chains, about true love *not* conquering all. (Note: dungeon represents a place of suffering, just as hell implies darkness and imprisonment. Guess what! The prince was in hell!) The prince being in this type of hell is a picture of Jesus descending into the lower parts of the earth (hell) to spoil and strip the enemy of everything he had stolen from God (Ephesians 4:9). When the good fairies reached the prince, they told him that they couldn't help him because the powers of the evil one were greater, but they could give him a shield of virtue and a sword of truth, which they called the weapons of righteousness, to help him triumph over evil.

Ephesians 6:10-17 confirms that the spiritual weapons given to the believer will help us do the same—triumph over evil. The *Helmet of Salvation* protects the mind from Satan's lies. We put on the *Breastplate of Righteousness* by reminding ourselves that God looks at us through Christ's righteousness; therefore, there is no condemnation when we do something wrong. We can repent and move on in our righteousness. We put on the *Belt of Truth* by learning the Bible truths so when the enemy attacks, we'll know the truth of God's Word, and the Word will hold us up. The *Sword of the Spirit* is God's Rhema Word, which He directly gives you pertaining to a particular trial. For example, if the enemy is attacking you in your marriage, and God has already given you a Word about that situation, you fight the enemy with that Word. Then strap on the *Shoes of the Gospel of Peace,* knowing that you can stand firm in the battle against Satan. Hold the *Shield of Faith* high by putting your trust in God for victory when Satan attacks and tries to defeat you. It means that you won't doubt what God says because you take Him at His Word and believe His promises. The scripture for the *Shield of Faith* says, "Above all, taking the shield of faith, wherewith ye shall be able to quench all the fiery darts of the wicked one" (v. 16).

After receiving these weapons from the good fairies, the prince proceeded to do exactly what they told him to do. When the ugly creatures came against him, he fought them off one by one. As each shot their fiery darts, when the darts hit his shield, the darts turned into flowers. The evil creatures pushed huge boulders off the top to crush the prince, but before the rocks could hit him, they turned into bubbles. Then, as the prince galloped on his horse towards the gate, they dropped hot melting lava at the gateway. But when a rainbow suddenly appeared over the exit, the lava didn't touch him. Do you see the protection and love of God when we use our spiritual weapons?

The prince finally made it out from the dungeon and away from the evil one, but she put up a barrier, a forest of thorns around the castle, so he couldn't reach

Sleeping Beauty, who was lying asleep in the castle. The prince began cutting and chopping and cutting and chopping his way through the thick forest of thorns—much as we must do as believers with the spiritual sword given to us. We must use the Word of God to cut down the cares of this world with which Satan tries to entrap us.

All of a sudden, the evil fairy turned into a dragon and told the prince that he would now have to deal with all the powers of hell. The fight was intense, and the dragon looked as if she was winning the battle. Although the prince was obviously exhausted and appeared to be overcome by his enemy, he continued to persevere and fight. He fell down and got back up and fell down and got back up. He even lost his shield. Then the fairies cast a blessing on the sword that evil would die and good would endure. He threw the sword at the dragon and it hit the mark. It struck the dragon in the heart.

What This Means for You

Just like the prince in this story, you may be in the midst of the worst battle of your life right now, and in that fight, it appears that you are losing. Just know that the Word is blessed when you don't doubt in your heart, and good will endure. You have already won! The victory is yours if you just hold onto God's Word and what He has spoken to you. We have confidence because our Prince of Peace has already come, died, and defeated the enemy. Because of His actions, we are destined to overcome and win whatever situation we may find ourselves in. We *will* triumph over the enemy.

Through this fight between the prince and the dragon, the Holy Spirit gave me a vivid picture of what our Prince, Jesus Christ, had to endure before ascending to the right hand of the Father. So we have to realize that it was only Jesus—not angels, not the Holy Spirit—no one but Jesus Himself who had to go to hell, defeat the devil, and save His beloved (you and me) from our sins. I could see Jesus, literally fighting Satan in the kingdom of darkness, destroying all the works of the devil, triumphing over sin and death, reclaiming everything that rightfully belonged to God, and reconciling mankind back to the Father. All that Jesus endured and the benefits of the price He paid on the cross are available to whosoever accepts Him as Lord and Savior of their lives. That is why the gates of hell cannot prevail against us because Jesus has already won the battle. Thank You, Jesus!

My Bible says that Jesus promises that the gates of hell shall not prevail against the church, which gives me a picture that the church is on the offensive and the devil is on the defensive. Since the devil has no authority over us, we can aggressively attack and snatch what belongs to us, including our loved ones, out of darkness into His glorious Kingdom of Light.

Immediately at the death of the dragon, the kingdom was no longer in darkness. The weeds and entanglement of the forest-like atmosphere were gone and the sun came out in all its brilliance and glory. The prince had beaten the evil one. The curse was now reversed. This scene demonstrates what happens when you first receive Christ as your Savior. Before coming to Jesus, your life is in total darkness and your heart is entangled in a forest of sin. Then you hear the message of the gospel and God's love immediately comes into your heart. The darkness that once clouded your life is now overpowered by the radiance and brilliance of God's glory—His presence. You are translated out of the kingdom of darkness and the enemy of your soul is defeated. You are now a born-again child of God. Thank You, Jesus!

The prince ran to his beloved, sealed his love for her with a kiss, and she was awakened with love in her heart. Instantly, all the people throughout the city were awakened, as well. The two were married and the two kingdoms were finally united as one and they lived happily ever after. Unlike this fable, however, when Jesus fought against Satan, that was only the beginning. He hadn't finished God's work. In order to unite the kingdoms—in order to allow all people to enter the Kingdom of Heaven—He had to seal it with His blood. Read Ephesians 2:11-22, but in verse 16 (AB) it says, "And [He designed] to reconcile to God both [Jew and Gentile, united] in a single body by means of His cross, thereby killing the mutual enmity and bringing the feud to an end."

Here are other reasons Jesus died: 1) that all people throughout the universe (Jews and Gentiles) could partake of God's love; and 2) to end the feud once and for all, so that God would always remain the God of heaven and earth.

In Ephesians 4:10, it says that Jesus died that He might fulfill all things. What are just a few of those things?

- that the whole universe would move from the lowest extreme (darkness/hell) to the highest (heaven/light);
- that sin would no longer dominate us because we have forgiveness;
- that Satan would be defeated; therefore, we now rule and reign over him;
- that we would no longer be subject to death because we have eternal life;
- that we were once powerless and now we have power;
- that no longer are we subject to the law because we now have grace;
- that we would have no fear because we live by faith; and
- that hatred would be substituted with love.

Of course, I could go on and on, but I'll stop here at His love. It was because of His love for you and me that Jesus gave His very life. God loved you and me so much that He manifested Himself in the flesh (remember the Word was God [John 1:1] and the Word [God] was made flesh [Jesus] [John 1:14]) and then He showed off His miraculous powers and wisdom on the earth, died on the cross, was buried, then resurrected.

Again, I just gave a few examples of what Jesus conquered and fulfilled. Now, I want to also show you a few things God had in mind when He allowed His Son to die for you and me. Through Jesus, we have:

His Divine Deliverance—"He personally bore our sins in His [own] body on the tree [as on an altar and offered Himself on it], that we might die (cease to exist) to sin and live to righteousness. By His wounds you have been healed" (1 Peter 2:24 AB).

His Faith—By faith we understand that the world was framed by the word of God; so then, faith cometh by hearing, and hearing by the Word of God (my paraphrase of Hebrews 11:3 and Romans 10:17).

His Grace—Jesus says, "My grace is sufficient for thee: for My strength is made perfect in weakness" (2 Corinthians 12:9).

His Spirit—"In whom ye also trusted, after that ye heard the word of truth, the gospel of your salvation: in whom also after that ye believed, ye were sealed with that Holy Spirit of promise" (Ephesians 1:13).

His Power—"According as his divine power hath given unto us all things that pertain unto life and godliness, through the knowledge of him that hath called us to glory and virtue" (2 Peter 1:3).

His Promises—"And if ye be Christ's, then are ye Abraham's seed, and heirs according to the promise" (Galatians 3:29).

His Love—"And hope maketh not ashamed; because the love of God is shed abroad in our hearts by the Holy Ghost which is given unto us" (Romans 5:5).

His Word—"In the beginning [before all time] was the Word (Christ), and the Word was with God, and the Word was God Himself" (John 1:1 AB).

His Forgiveness—"If we confess our sins, he is faithful and just to forgive us our sins, and to cleanse us from all unrighteousness" (1 John 1:9).

His Life—"Verily, verily, I say unto you, He that believeth on me, the works that I do shall he do also; and greater works than these shall he do; because I go unto my Father" (John 14:12).

His Blessings—"Blessed be the God and Father of our Lord Jesus Christ, who hath blessed us with all spiritual blessings in heavenly places in Christ" (Ephesians 1:3).

The question I have for you is this: Why did He die if we don't experience God's love and live in what He left for us? Paul simply puts it like this: "I don't want to frustrate my God by not accepting His grace: for if who I am is by a law, then Christ died in vain" (my

15

paraphrase of Galatians 2:21). People of God, accept the precious Gift God gave us—His love through Jesus' death on the cross.

God wants you to fully understand…

> [that you may really come] to know [practically through experience for yourselves] the love of Christ, which far surpasses mere knowledge [without experience]; that you may be filled [through all your being] unto all the fullness of God [may have the richest measure of the divine Presence, and become a body wholly filled and flooded with God Himself]! (Ephesians 3:19 AB)

This is what Jesus did for you and me! Hallelujah! God/Christ in us—we are flooded with Him on the inside of us when we gave our life to Him. No longer do we need prophets and/or priests to go to God for us. Because there is one God, and one mediator between God and men, the man Christ Jesus (1 Timothy 2:5), we now have access to God directly, just as Adam and Eve did before they sinned.

Again, our marriages should reflect Jesus' love for the church. Everything God does is motivated by love. Jesus' life exemplifies love for mankind. He gave His very life for us. I know for sure that you, the reader, did not go to the depths of hell to fight Satan. Nor were you beaten so bad that people couldn't recognize you. Nor were you mocked with a thorn of crowns on your head or nails driven through your hands on a cross. Nor were you buried and resurrected on the third day. Now that is love! God is love, and we are created in His image and likeness. Therefore, the love He freely gave you, you should give to others. The forgiveness He freely gave you, you should give to others. The blessings He freely gave you, you should give to others. Do you get the point?

Beloved, let us love one another: for love is of God; and every one that loveth is born of God, and knoweth God. He that loveth not knoweth not God; for God is love. In this was manifested the love of God toward us, because that God sent his only begotten Son into the world, that we might live through him. Herein is love, not that we loved God, but that he loved us, and sent his Son *to be* the propitiation for our sins. Beloved, if God so loved us, we ought also to love one another. No man hath seen God at any time. If we love one another, God dwelleth in us, and his love is perfected in us. Hereby know we that we dwell in him, and he in us, because he hath given us of his Spirit. And we have seen and do testify that the Father sent the Son *to be* the Saviour of the world. Whosoever shall confess that Jesus is the Son of God, God dwelleth in him, and he in God.

And we have known and believed the love that God hath to us. God is love; and he that dwelleth in love dwelleth in God, and God in him. Herein is our love made perfect, that we may have boldness in the day of judgment: because as he is [love—*my addition*], so are we [love—*my addition*] in this world. (1 John 4:7-17)

Jesus gave us all we need to have a successful marriage. Let's use all His wisdom and love to develop and nurture the very special gift He gave us: our spouses. All that you need is the greater One on the inside of you. Let's honor Jesus' love by demonstrating His love to others, especially our spouses.

Chapter 1

Wake Up, Sleeping Beauty!
Marriage Is No Fairy Tale

But refuse profane and old wives' fables, and exercise thyself *rather* unto godliness. For bodily exercise profiteth little: but godliness is profitable unto all things. (1 Timothy 4:7-8)

As I was growing up, I read all the fairytale books like Sleeping Beauty, hoping one day to meet my prince and live happily ever after. However, most fairytales give us an unrealistic picture of what our life with the prince will be like. Just like Cinderella, who met her prince at a ball and he came looking for her with a glass slipper, and when he found her, they lived happily ever after; you, too, will marry and have a fairytale ending, right? That is certainly what I had pictured for my life. You know, Jewell sees Lewis from afar and is awed by his handsome presence. One day as she is waiting to buy lunch, she turns around and bumps right into her Prince Charming. They eat together and fall madly in love. They get married and live happily ever after. Well . . . not quite.

Between falling in love and getting married, Lewis and I sought God's guidance and attended an extensive premarital counseling class for three-and-a-half months. The pastor stressed two things that I now know are so important: (1) that couples attend the same church so they are receiving the same teaching and are of the same faith, and (2) that combined finances are in the black before they get married. He also added that we shouldn't set a date for the wedding before counseling because people aren't totally honest with their feelings, especially if they have already put a down payment on a reception area, videographers, and other wedding expenses.

After counseling, couples should be 100 percent sure that they belong together before proceeding. If you do that, you will be able to weather the storms in your marriage much better when they arise.

And they *will* arise. All couples go through some storms, and your marriage will not be exempt. If you realize this at the beginning, you won't separate or divorce because of false expectations or doubts about whether your spouse is right for you. Instead, when you go through trials and tribulations, you will believe that you are supposed to be with your mate, and therefore you will be willing to do what it takes to make your marriage work. I wish I wasn't giving this advice in hindsight—I should have given *myself* this advice beforehand (although I was and still am 100 percent sure Lewis and I belong together).

My Storm

I fell in love with a wonderful man. Lewis was literally everything I wanted in a man. I had written a list of characteristics I wanted in my husband, and I placed this sheet of paper in my Bible and prayed. When I met Lewis, I prayed constantly and asked God for confirmation on three different occasions, and God confirmed each time that he was good for me. In fact, the last time, God told me to take out my list and see for myself! Lewis had everything on that list (which consisted of about twenty-five characteristics) minus the two from which he was seeking deliverance. As I'm writing this book ten years later, he is actually more than I asked for. Praise God, His Word is true, for doing exceedingly and abundantly above what I can ask or think (Ephesians 3:20)!

We dated for four years before we got married, and I knew without a shadow of doubt that my marriage was ordained by God. When we went through the storm, I still knew in my heart that he was for me, but the devil kept whispering, "You can do better. You don't have to take this." I thought, "I was all right before I met him, and I will be all right when he is gone." My thoughts were stupid! I couldn't do better because I had the best man for me. Although Lewis is not perfect, he is the perfect person *for me*. And I am not perfect either. I may be a perfectionist, but I am not perfect. I hope you can face that truth about yourself as well, and say it out loud: "I _____(fill in your name) am not perfect and neither is _____(fill in your better half)." Good! Hopefully, confessing it will be a start to a happily-ever-after-marriage.

How did Lewis and I go from "perfect for each other" to "you can do better"? When we married in

May 1996, we were the best of friends and got along extremely well. We had some issues, and some pet peeves, but the bottom line was that we knew that God had put us together for a reason. One month into our marriage, though, we started arguing, and as time wore on, the arguments got worse. Sometimes we could go weeks, even months, without arguing; but when we argued, we *argued*. I felt that he wasn't spending enough time with me. He loved to work, and still does, but in my eyes he worked too much. I could have seen this as something great: I had a man who worked hard to take care of his family. But I complained instead. I couldn't see that I was trying to substitute him for something that was missing in my life.

When I got married, I lost practically all my friends. In hindsight, God had separated me from them to draw me closer to Him. Therefore, Lewis was the only person I had to talk to or do anything with. I needed him to give me more time because I didn't have anyone else. So my marriage started falling apart right at the beginning because I was looking to Lewis to fulfill me in areas that were now vacant. I eventually learned that God is the only one who can supply all my needs (Philippians 4:19). If I am unfulfilled, it is not because of my spouse, children, friends, or job. I put that weight on Lewis, which was wrong! Psalm 118:8 says, "It is better to trust and take refuge in the Lord than to put confidence in man" (AB). Now I am not troubled by what Lewis does or doesn't do because my expectation is in God. I go to Him first, and He will direct Lewis or whomever to do what is needed for me.

As David wrote, "My soul, wait thou only upon God; for my expectation is from him" (Psalm 62:5).

We also argued about finances. Lewis is a saver, and I am a spender. (I am still working on that part!) So he kept his money separate from mine. I started hearing "your money, my money." I used to get so mad because as a couple, it's *our* money. I didn't like him telling me that I couldn't buy the things I wanted (not needed). I worked hard every day. I thought I deserved nice things for me and my house. Again, my thoughts were out of order. If I had been submissive, we would be stronger financially by now. But I thought he was punishing me.

Then we argued about children. I wanted to adopt first, and Lewis wanted his own first. After three years of marriage and not being able to conceive (and after three years of arguing about whose fault that was), he finally agreed to foster care. We eventually adopted our foster child and afterwards conceived our own child. Guess what? Even then, we still argued. We argued about how to raise the kids. I am the disciplinary parent; he is not. Then there were the arguments that came before and after I became a stay-at-home mom. He could not understand why I needed a break and time to myself.

It went on and on, and we are still dealing with issues even now. But glory be to God, we handle them a lot differently than we used to. I seek God as to what I should say and whether I should even say anything at all. Now our disagreements and challenges bring us closer to one another instead of dividing us, as they did before.

Life or Death

I made another mistake in the beginning of my marriage, and it wasn't even a conscious thing. It was something I observed from my parents. My mother and father used to play a little game about "Jody," my mother's imaginary boyfriend. When my mother was out all day, my father would always ask her if she had been with Jody, and she would playfully say "yes." I brought that game into my marriage, and it caused a lot of confusion and arguments. Lewis even took it a step further. He came up with "Jodette," his pretend girlfriend.

God rebuked me for starting that because we have power to speak life and death into our marriages (see Proverbs 18:21). I wasn't speaking life; I was speaking death—adultery. I was just playing, but the devil was waiting to use what we said. Never give the devil a chance to sneak in and seize an opportunity. Lewis and I promised to never speak those names again as long as we live. Make sure you are at all times speaking life into your marriage. Don't say one day, "I love you, Baby; you are the best thing that ever happened to me," and the next day tell your spouse, "I hate you; you make me sick, and I wish I never married you." You just spoke death.

I now think of my mouth as a compass. What comes out of it directs my relationship. For example, if I am going to have a heavenly marriage, I need to speak in that direction. If something is about to come out that would change my marriage to go south (straight to hell), I don't say it. Anything contrary to

24

the Word of God directs it hellward. I had to change the direction of my marriage since it was moving toward adultery. I now confess that my husband wants no one but me, and I don't want anyone but him. Amen.

As you can see, once Lewis and I got married, all hell broke loose. We had one argument after another. They started off so small, but the ball kept rolling. Why? Because we never truly sought God's answers to our problems. We didn't seek Him concerning how we should communicate or what we should say. God will answer all questions, both small and large. His Word says for us to cast *all our cares* on Him (1 Peter 5:7). Often, we try not to rock the boat; but this leaves trouble unresolved, brewing on the inside and waiting for another opportunity to blow up. However, if we seek God and His answers and handle the problem accordingly, we can resolve the situation and not have something on the inside waiting to erupt. Therefore, get on your knees and pray for the Lord to direct your mouth, thoughts, and actions. He will give you the wisdom to say just the right thing to turn that problem around. Since Lewis and I reconciled, when potential conflicts arise, the Holy Spirit will tell me to just shut up, to apologize even if I am right, and/or the exact thing to say that will stop the argument right in its tracks.

Don't Quit

You may be at a place where you just can't take any more. You say, "I've been with this man for two months, a year, a couple of years, and *I can't take any more!*" You are ready to throw your marriage away, which means you are ready for separation or divorce. Don't do it; don't give up! The Bible says, "What *God has joined* together, let not man separate" (Matthew 19:6 NIV). You may have thought you chose your mate. But God has joined the two of you together. Even though you may believe you chose the wrong one, God already knew you were going to marry that particular person and He can still use your mistakes for His good. God honors all marriages, whether you think you made a mistake or not. God says *no man* (or *woman*) should separate the married couple; and that includes *you*, the one who is about to give up. Don't give up!

In February 2001, my husband and I hit rock bottom after four-and-a-half years of marriage. I hoped a marriage conference would help us, so I asked him to commit to going for the three days. Again, my first mistake was putting my expectation in him and not going to God and having Him deal with Lewis' commitment. The first day, we attended the night session, and I realized that the turnaround in my marriage started with me. I needed to change, and the beauty of it was that I was ready to change. The next day, we went to the day sessions, but during the evening session, we literally argued throughout the entire time (quietly though). I was ready to give up and was tired of arguing with my husband, tired of him not acting right, tired of him not spending time with me and the girls, tired of him not going to church, tired of him hanging out with the wrong people and doing the wrong things. Just tired of being tired. I didn't feel that

26

we were headed in the same direction. We left the church in separate cars and did not speak to one another at all. By the way, we had been sleeping in separate rooms for months. The last day, Lewis didn't show up for the day sessions, and I cried throughout the whole service because I was at the end of my rope.

Here I was, getting God's Word, yet so miserable. All I kept hearing was, "Don't give up!" I kept saying to myself, "It is over"; however, I kept listening and hearing God say, "Don't give up!" At the end of those sessions, I told my pastor that the Word was awesome and that what was preached literally changed my life. I was excited about what was going to happen in my marriage as a result of this conference. I went home and called Lewis about the evening session and he said he wasn't going.

I would like to think that I am a woman who is filled and controlled by the Holy Spirit, but I lost it. I told him to pack his bags and that he had one hour. I now know what it feels like to be temporarily insane. My heart was broken. I was hurting so bad. I thought if he didn't care about this marriage, I wasn't going to fight for it anymore. I felt that I had been fighting for years now. The main reason we were still together was because I was fighting. However, hindsight says that I was never fighting. I was nagging, complaining, and judging him. Also, I was trying to repair a messed-up marriage in my own strength. I was fighting a battle that could only be won with Jesus.

When we are struggling with something, it's probably because we haven't allowed God to help correct the situation. When I completely submitted to the Lord and all He told me to do, I was at peace. I wasn't struggling and wasn't unhappy. Although God had to work on Lewis, and although Lewis may have made my life less peaceful, it didn't phase me. The only thing I was supposed to do was change. It all started with me, and God told me not to worry about Lewis and what he was or was not doing.

When Lewis left on that cold and rainy day to stay in a hotel, the warfare started in my mind. The devil steadily whispered, "You are going to be okay. You were okay before him and you will be okay after him." But my spirit was saying, "You know what you did was wrong. You know you are supposed to be with this man. This is your husband, the father of your children. You know you were not supposed to throw him out of his house. You are being taught the Word and are supposed to be a doer of the Word. But you are dishonoring Me, smacking Me in My face and saying, "Yes, Lord, I heard your Word, but I just don't want to do what I know is right."

I was in even deeper sorrow because I knew that I hurt my Heavenly Father, and I knew better. God told me to fix it. I had to do whatever it took to get Lewis back home because God was not pleased with my actions. God told me to call him that night. Of course, he didn't answer the phone, so I left a message that I loved him. That phone call started us toward reconciliation.

Seeing Beyond the Natural

How did I get to that place of separation? In hindsight, God showed me that I was focusing too much on the horizontal relationship (between Lewis and me) and not enough on the vertical relationship (between my Heavenly Father and me). I was putting too much effort, work, and thought toward my husband. I needed to work on me, praying to the Father and developing a deeper relationship with Him. It was not my place, nor my responsibility, to change Lewis—that was God's job. Some of you may be thinking, "I'm not trying to change my spouse." Well, anything you think your spouse is or is not doing to your satisfaction is trying to change that person. I was trying to be God. The Lord, however, told me that He did not need my help. He is God, and He can do all things by Himself. I was out of line, out of position, and out of control.

Throughout the whole reconciliation process, I was seeking God with my whole heart, asking question after question. He answered every last one of them. One day, the Lord spoke through my pastor and gave me something that was profound. Pastor Tony said, "We look at our children and spouses in the flesh to the point that we see them as ours." Pastor Tony went on to say that they are ours in the sense that God has blessed us with these individuals; they are a gift from God. But do we own them? No. God owns everything and everyone on this earth (Psalm 24:1). He bestowed His blessing on us in that He gave us a spouse and children. Who are we to look at our spouse and

29

children in the flesh and not see them as the man, woman, or child God is calling them to be?

I learned to stop looking at my family in the flesh and to start seeing them through the eyes of Christ. They may not be where God has called them to be, but you don't know what God has planned for them one, two, five, or ten years from now. I didn't see Lewis beyond what he was in the flesh; so I was focusing on his faults and problems. In 2 Corinthians 5:16, God says, "Consequently, from now on we estimate and regard no one from a [purely] human point of view—in terms of natural standards of value" (AB). Bottom line, don't look at them in the flesh, but see them from God's perspective.

How do we do that? Begin by paying attention to what you say to your spouse. If you hear yourself saying things like, "God wants you to start going to church, God wants you to stop smoking, God wants you to stop going to clubs," then you are looking at the flesh and what your mate is currently doing. In effect, you are judging and condemning your spouse, and this does not please God. God is working on that man or woman, and that man is going to be a mighty man of valor or that woman is going to become a virtuous woman in due season. We need to look at our spouses in light of what God has called them to be and the works He is doing through them. We should not go by what we see today, for we walk by faith and not by sight (2 Corinthians 5:7). The proper view of your mate comes from the Word.

So what does the Word of God say about your man or woman of God? It says that he is a man who loves

30

his wife as Christ loves the church, so your husband will love you that way one day. It says she speaks of wisdom and her husband and children will call her blessed, so she will be that way one day.

However, that will not happen if you don't continue to pray for and speak those things (Mark 11:24). When Lewis and I were going through difficult times in our marriage, all I saw and talked about were negative things. I was looking at him in his flesh and concentrating more on those fleshly characteristics than on the positive things that would have shown him as the man of God he is. I believe that if you ask God to reveal to you your man or woman of God, He will open your (spiritual) eyes immediately.

So as you can see, I was literally Sleeping Beauty. I had no clue as to what marriage was about or my role in it until Lewis and I separated and I started seeking God for answers. Throughout the reconciliation process, God was showing me His plan and purpose and how my marriage could be happily ever after—if I did it His way. Remember, His way is perfect.

Let's pray:

Father, in the name of Jesus, I ask for Your help so that I may change and become all that You have called me to be and do. Create in me a clean heart and renew a right spirit in me. Direct me Lord, so that my marriage will be happily ever after, which will glorify You. In Jesus' name. Amen.

Chapter 2
Good Fairies

But the Comforter, which is the Holy Ghost, whom the Father will send in my name, he shall teach you all things, and bring all things to your remembrance, whatsoever I have said unto you. (John 14:26)

In Sleeping Beauty's story, the good fairies had magical powers and pronounced blessings over the princess. God, of course, is not a magician; but He gave us the Holy Spirit, who guides us and directs us into all truth. God has given us certain roles in life, and He explains how we should fulfill them in His Word. The Holy Spirit helps us to carry out God's plan and purpose for our lives when we call on Him. So why is it so difficult for us to do what He says in His Word? Maybe because we have our own ideas and purposes that are not in line with God's.

Single State

I need to deal with singleness because, hopefully, some people will read this book before they get married. In Genesis 1:27, it says, "God created man in his image, male and female created he them." We need

33

to understand God's plan as far as order. He knew from the beginning that He was going to create male and female. God created everything in the world before He made the very good thing: man. Man was made to take care of, and be in charge of, all that was created. Therefore, God put him in a position (job) first. Adam's job was to name all the animals and till the ground.

Women, there is a reason men take so long to ask for your hand in marriage. Men need to get things in order (career, education, money in the bank) before they take on the responsibility of a wife. So where did men get this? They got it from Adam. God made Adam first, to get things prepared before his wife. That is why she is a "helpmeet": she helps him in his job. Women, if you are not willing to change your life and your plans by submitting to your man of God and his plans, don't get married. Being single means you can do what you want when you want. If you have goals you want to achieve, do them. Also, use this time to develop a deeper relationship with God. God wants you, at this stage, to become that whole person who is fulfilled and happy so that when you do get married, you don't have to seek fulfillment from your mate because you already bring it into the marriage.

Another reason a man may take awhile is that he is not ready to leave mama. As the Bible says, "Therefore shall a man leave his father and his mother, and shall cleave unto his wife" (Genesis 2:24). Deciding to marry is a big decision for a man to make. He is totally responsible for another human being. When Adam and Eve ate from the forbidden tree, they both were in trouble, but Adam took more of a punishment because he was responsible for his wife. In Genesis 3:11, God said to Adam, "Who told you that you were naked? Have you eaten from the tree that I commanded you not to eat from?" In verse 17, He told Adam, "Because you listened to your wife . . . cursed is the ground because of you; through painful toil you will eat of it all the days of your life" (NIV).

The Bible says that, before their fall into sin, Adam and Eve were both naked and were not ashamed. To me, that describes the core of the word *intimacy*. They saw each other as God saw them (notice that, afterwards, they saw each other in the flesh and covered themselves in shame). In genuine intimacy, I am not trying to change this man. I see him for who he is. I am not ashamed of who he is or what he does. And I can show him myself at my weakest point and not fear that he will use it against me.

When I was in the hospital for four months, I was totally bedridden. I couldn't get up to go to the bathroom or even take a shower. I was completely in the hands of the nurses and Lewis. I believe that experience was the most intimate yet grueling time in our marriage. My husband took care of me like no other person in this world would ever do. It wasn't a time for me to be embarrassed or ashamed. However, before that, there were things that I wouldn't do because I was embarrassed. My husband never saw the real me until then and probably would never have if it hadn't been for that circumstance.

Intimacy is more than sex; it is a deep inner connection—souls are connected when you are not ashamed. So don't hide your deepest secrets and fears from your potential mates. Let them see what your weaknesses are so they can cover them when crises arise.

Shame is a big part of the problem. We put on an act and lie to each other because we are ashamed of who we are. We go into relationships fearing that the person we love won't love us if he or she knows our secrets. Guess what? When we do this, we are already in the hands of Satan. If you don't open up to your potential mate now, then later on you will be wondering why you're having so many problems in your marriage. The devil just used what you started off with as a weapon to destroy your marriage. For those who are not yet married, this is a perfect opportunity to show your worst and then your best. If the person stays with you at your worst, he or she will be there always.

Marriage is work. It is probably the hardest yet most rewarding thing you will ever do. My husband told me that on our wedding day his brother (who was married) told him that this could be the best thing or the worst thing he would do. I was told that both of them were in the back room crying like babies for half an hour while I was waiting and wondering why the wedding hadn't started. But Lewis' brother was right. You can have a marriage of hell or of heaven. A heavenly marriage is going to take a lot of work. If you are not willing to put the work into having a long-lasting, until-you-die-marriage, you do not need to get married.

Role of the Husband

Men need to do three important things: (1) be the head of the household, (2) honor their woman of God, and (3) love their woman of God.

First Corinthians 11:3 says that the head of the woman is man. The word *head* indicates responsibility and accountability. Being the head does not mean superiority, nor does it give a right to be dictatorial or demanding. When a decision cannot be reached, the man makes the final decision. Men, women are looking to you to lead them in truth, the Word of God. Men, you are subject to authority as well—you are held accountable to Christ regarding your actions, words, thoughts, and behavior.

In case you didn't know, you are also to submit to your wife (Ephesians 5:21). You ask, "Why do I submit to her?" Out of reverence for Christ. See her as a woman of God who is like Christ on the earth, and treat her and talk to her as if Christ were in the room with you. Honor her by treating her with consideration and respect on the basis of shared faith. The Apostle Paul counseled:

> Husbands, love your wives, as Christ loved the church and gave Himself up for her, that He might sanctify her, having cleansed her by the washing of water with the Word, that He might present the church to Himself in glorious splendor—woman is the glory of man—without spot or wrinkle or any

such things [that she might be holy and faultless]. Even so husbands should love their wives as [being in a sense] their own bodies. He who loves his own wife loves himself. (Ephesians 5:25-28 AB)

How should you love your wife? Verse 29 says to nourish (to foster the development of; promote) and carefully protect and cherish her. Men, you will see other things throughout the book that you must do. But for now, know that you are ultimately responsible and held accountable for your family. Therefore, if nothing else, the man of God must know the Word of God.

Role of a Wife

Women need to do three important things: (1) reverence their man of God, (2) submit to their man of God, and (3) be a helpmeet to their man of God. God wants women to meditate on 1 Peter 3:1-8. If you read this by the leading of the Holy Spirit, you will understand that to do this is to walk before God with a pure heart and be a woman after God's own heart. In the Amplified, it says:

In like manner, you married women, be submissive to your own husbands [subordinate yourselves as being secondary to and dependent on them, and adapt yourselves to them], so that even if any do not obey the Word [of

38

God], they may be won over not by discussion but by the [godly] lives of their wives, when they observe the pure and modest way in which you conduct yourselves, together with your reverence [for your husband; you are to feel for him all that reverence includes: to respect, defer to, revere him—to honor, esteem, appreciate, prize and, in the human sense, to adore him, that is, to admire, praise, be devoted to, deeply love, and enjoy your husband]. Let not yours be the [merely] external adorning with [elaborate] interweaving and knotting of the hair, the wearing of jewelry, or change of clothes; but let it be the inward adorning and beauty of the hidden person of the heart, with the incorruptible and unfading charm of a gentle and peaceful spirit, which [is not anxious or wrought up, but] is very precious in the sight of God. For it was thus that the pious women of old who hoped in God were [accustomed] to beautify themselves and were submissive to their husbands [adapting themselves to them as themselves secondary and dependent upon them].

I must interject here: Forget what you have been taught about being independent and not depending on anyone. That is not God's way. You can still be who

God has called you to be while obeying the Word of God. In 1 Corinthians 11:11, the Word says, "Nevertheless, in [the plan of] the Lord and from His point of view woman is not apart from and independent of man, nor is man aloof from and independent of woman" (AB). I wasn't programmed biblically when I got married. My independence made my husband feel as though I really didn't need him. It got so bad that I started to think I really didn't... until he was gone. Women need to know that it is very important for men to feel needed. That's what reverencing our husbands accomplishes.

Back in 1 Peter:

> It was thus that Sarah obeyed Abraham [following his guidance and acknowledging his headship over her by] calling him lord [master, leader, authority]. And you are now her true daughters if you do right and let nothing terrify you [not giving way to hysterical fears or letting anxieties unnerve you]. (v. 6 AB)

Reverencing our husbands is so important. I remember one day, when Lewis and I were talking. I wasn't paying him much attention, and he threw out how I listen so attentively to my pastor, hanging onto every word that he preaches, and yet I can't seem to listen to him with the same attentiveness. Though his work may sometimes seem boring to me, I need to listen. That is another way we can reverence our

40

husbands. We can also let them know how important they are and how much we and the kids really need them. When Lewis walks through the door, the girls get so excited, screaming, "Daddy!" and jumping up and down. Sometimes I do the same thing! I know it makes his hard day great to have all his girls light up like Christmas trees when he walks in the door.

Here are some other ideas to make your man of God feel special: Fix him a candlelight dinner or breakfast in bed. Read between the lines and help him with something even though he didn't ask (taking out the trash, mowing the lawn). Call him up and ask, "What does my man of God want for dinner?" These are just little ways we can reverence our husbands. At a mom's meeting, one lady said that her husband likes having a pedicure. That is so awesome, because if Jesus could wash His disciples' feet, surely we can wash our husbands' feet!

Proverbs 31 is about a mother telling her son the type of woman he should seek. This is the type of woman we should emulate. We have probably read Proverbs 31 a million times. But every time we read it, we should get new revelation. Wherever we are in life, it will apply. When I read it for the first time, I read it from a wife's perspective. When my husband asked me to come home to take care of the children, I read it from a homemaker's viewpoint. As I was contemplating whether to start a home-based business, I read it from a businesswoman's point of view. And when I started seeking God diligently, I read it simply as a woman of God. So this one passage applies in a lot of different ways.

As women of God, we need to strive to be virtuous women. We need to be guided and directed by the Word of God. As Christian women filled with the Holy Spirit, we need to be controlled by the Holy Spirit at all times. Therefore, our reserve of the Word of God should never run low. God says that His people perish because they lack knowledge (see Hosea 4:6). Being filled with the Word helps us to be all that God has called us to be, whether we're a spouse, an employee, or a friend.

Therefore, women, keep your tongue under control. I know that my tongue used to be lethal. I would say things that I knew would hurt my husband or anyone else. But Proverbs 31 says that when I open my mouth, the law of kindness should be on my tongue (v. 26). When we decided to accept Jesus into our lives, we also accepted the responsibilities that go with that. Therefore, we must read the Word and do what it says. Our responsibility to God is to show Him on the earth. God is love, and there is no evil in Him. Therefore, honor Him in every word that is spoken.

In summary, the wife's role is that of an enabler, a cheerleader, and a helper. She should be trustworthy and dependable while edifying and building up her husband at all times.

Virtuous Women

Again, Proverbs 31 talks of all the qualities of a virtuous woman. One verse states that "her children arise up, and call her blessed; her husband also, and he praiseth her" (v. 28). Our men of God should be calling us blessed and praising us. Is your husband calling you blessed? Does he praise you? If not, is there something you are not doing that you should?

In the book of Ruth, Ruth's fiancé, Boaz, told her that his whole city knew that she was a virtuous woman (3:11). Why was she virtuous? Ruth was a Moabite (and, research says, a king's daughter). She was married to one of Naomi's sons for about ten years. When Ruth's husband and brother-in-law died, her mother-in-law (Naomi) wanted to return to her people, the Israelites. Naomi tried to get Ruth and her sister-in-law to stay with their own people and their own gods, but Ruth insisted on going with Naomi. When Ruth's husband died, she had no reason to leave Moab. Yet she left because, in her eyes, she was no longer a Moabite. She was an Israelite who took on her husband's name and all that came with it. "And Ruth said, Urge me not to leave you or to turn back from following you; for where you go I will go, and where you lodge I will lodge. Your people shall be my people and your God my God" (Ruth 1:16 AB).

I received several revelations from reading this book. First, Ruth's mother-in-law was a woman of God. Ruth saw God in Naomi; that is why she wanted to follow her and her God. Second, she totally gave herself to her husband in name, heritage, religion, and spirit. Again, she was no longer a king's daughter or a Moabite. How many of us have kept our maiden names because we thought we would lose our identity? You don't lose anything; you gain it when it comes to God's way of doing things. Once in Bethlehem, Ruth (a king's daughter) immediately went out to work because they were not well off. If we were in her shoes, just think of the attitude most of us would have. In fact, let's bring it closer to home. Say your husband wants to start a janitorial service and wants you to come work for him. Would you think that this kind of work is beneath you? Or try this one: You went to graduate school, have a career you love, and a very nice salary, but your husband wants you to leave to take care of the children and home. What would you say? "How dare you ask me to be a stay-at-home mom!" Oops, that one hurt! Trust God and your man of God.

Throughout life, seek God's plan and not your own. After leaving a career of twelve years, I realized that it was all part of God's plan for me to be where I am today. Because Ruth followed her mother-in-law, she ended up marrying a wealthy man and her son was the grandfather of David, the ancestor of Jesus.

Ruth is the only woman in the Bible called a virtuous woman. I believe it was because she took on the identity of her husband and followed after the things of God. For example, if you are a Jehovah's Witness and you married a Christian, you need to take on your husband's identity, Christianity. Again, if you look at it as a loss, you may hold up what God has for you. The reasons you take on his identity are: (1) your children's heritage comes from the father, (2) you need to honor your husband, and (3) so you can to receive all that God has for you (it's His will). However, if you're a Christian and married to an unbeliever (i.e. a Muslim or a Hindu), you should pray for your spouse. There is hope if you believe in the Word of God: "For surely there is a latter end [a future and a reward], and

your hope and expectation shall not be cut off"
(Proverbs 23:18 AB).

Women of Influence

In Genesis 3, the serpent tempted Eve. Eve told
him that they couldn't eat from the tree in the middle
of the garden. But when she saw the tree, it was good
and delightful to look at. She ate and gave some to her
husband to eat. As helpmeets to our husbands, we need
to walk by faith and not by sight. We simply need to
have the heart of our spouse, which means being
faithful men and women of God who do the Word by
any means necessary. When Eve heard from the devil,
she should have said, "No, my husband told me that
we should not eat from the tree, so we won't." As men
and women after God's own heart, let's just decide to
be led by the Holy Spirit and stand on the Word no
matter what it looks like.

Just a short mention of Sarah. She was a good wife
in that she knew Abraham was lord over her life. Yes, I
said *lord*. He is the little *l*, not the big *L*. They stayed
married until her death. Abraham told her what God
revealed to him in a vision. Unfortunately, she took it
upon herself to accomplish it, giving her maid to sleep
with her husband to have children. Her faith wasn't
strong because she had not sought after God herself.
Genesis 16:2 says, "Abram hearkened to the voice of
Sarai," which we know was the wrong thing to do.
There are three voices: (1) Jesus', (2) yours, and (3)
the devil's. Jesus says, "My sheep know my voice and
the voice of a stranger they shall not follow" (John

10:4-5). We should always want to do what's right in the sight of God toward our mates; therefore, follow the voice of Jesus.

As women, we need to be women of influence—positive influence. Eve and Sarah were women of influence, but in the wrong way. My opinion is that they didn't have a relationship with God for themselves; it was only through their husbands. Each of us needs to have our own relationship with God. Ruth was a woman of positive influence, and she inherited a good life. Queen Esther is another woman in the Bible who was a woman of positive influence, and she saved her people from destruction. Women of positive influence are women who are submissive, who have a relationship with God and therefore have an ear to hear from Him, and who know the will of God for their lives. You may not know the will of God for your marriage right now, but know that He has a plan.

Marriage

According to Matthew 1:21, Jesus was born to save us from our sins. In God's Word, He said He knew us from the beginning of the earth, before we were in our mother's womb. God knows all; He knew that you would grow up and get married one day so that you would fulfill His purpose and perfect plan here on earth.

What is marriage? Marriage is a covenant (a pledge, vow, promise, or agreement made between two parties to carry out the terms agreed upon). It cannot (or should not) be terminated until the death of a spouse. Therefore, when you got married, you made a covenant commitment to God that you would do the words you spoke and that you would let Him have His way in your marriage; it is His institution after all. Psalm 89:34 states, "My covenant will I not break, nor alter the thing that is gone out of my lips." If you want God to keep His covenant with you, you must keep yours with Him. If you don't, your offerings (praise and worship, tithes and offerings, blessings and honor, and/or your seeking of forgiveness) may be rejected. Keep this in perspective. Although God is a loving and forgiving God, you cannot go before Him with your offerings without having repented for how you've been treating your spouse and/or not having changed your ways.

As the prophet Malachi said:

Yet you ask, Why does He reject [the offering]? Because the Lord was witness [to the covenant made at your marriage] between you and the wife of your youth, against whom you have dealt treacherously and to whom you were faithless. Yet she is your companion and the wife of your covenant [made by your marriage vows]. And did not God make [you and your wife] one [flesh]? Did not One make you and preserve your spirit alive? And why [did God make you two] one? Because He sought a godly offspring [from your union]. Therefore

take heed to yourselves, and let no one
deal treacherously and be faithless to
the wife of his youth. For the Lord, the
God of Israel, says: I hate divorce and
marital separation and him who covers
his garment [his wife] with violence.
(Malachi 2:14-16 AB)

The two become one—two different individuals
with vast differences and desires have agreed to come
together as one. They have shared desires, goals,
dreams, and plans, and are connected spiritually. Both
men and women are to submit themselves one to
another in the fear of God, asking their mates, "What
can I do for you?" or "How can I help you today?" I
was taught in premarital class to have this attitude (and
mean it): *I live to please my man (or woman) of God.* I
tell Lewis that all the time. It is the simplest way to
submit to one another, just doing those things you
know will please them.

As I mentioned in Chapter 1, all hell broke loose in
my marriage because I was neglecting God. I wasn't
developing my relationship with Him because I was
too focused on my natural relationship with my
husband. I didn't seek answers from God until the
trials and tribulations came. For those of us who have
children, you know how, as they become young adults,
they think they know the game of life. They don't seek
answers from you because they think they know it all.
That is how most of us are when we get married. God
and His Word are nowhere in sight. He is the One who
created the marriage covenant; therefore, since He

48

knows all, why wouldn't you ask Him on a daily basis how to deal with your spouse? Proverbs 3:5-6 says, "Trust in the Lord with all thine heart, and lean not unto thine own understanding. In all thy ways acknowledge him, and he shall direct thy paths." We need, on a daily basis, to seek God regarding how we are to accomplish things pertaining to all of our relationships.

> *Father, in the name of Jesus, I ask You to change me. Today I make a quality decision to do Your will and do it Your way. I will take my eyes and thoughts off my spouse and turn myself over to You. Do a work in me that would help me become a better wife/husband. For I am Your workmanship, created in Christ Jesus for good works, which You have planned beforehand, that we should walk in them, living the good life that you have prearranged and made ready for us to live. I know that it is possible, because with You all things are possible. Thank You in Jesus' name, Amen.*

It really is not hard to change or to do the things discussed in this book. In 1 Corinthians 11:1, Paul writes that we should follow his example because he imitated Christ. The Bible gives us an example, Jesus, of how we can do the things our Father has written for us to do. Jesus had to die so the Comforter, the Holy

Spirit, could come and dwell on the inside of every born again Christian to comfort us, help us, and guide us throughout our lives. Just know that when you make the decision to do God's will, the devil will do all he can to stop your process of change.

Chapter 3

Evil Fairy

Be sober, be vigilant; because your adversary the devil, as a roaring lion, walketh about, seeking whom he may devour. (1 Peter 5:8)

The devil and evil spirits are real. They want you to do everything that is contrary to the Word of God, the things of God, and the people of God. This is how, when your mate does something you don't like, you become offended. This is how you can come out of church and argue all the way home. This is how you can make a decision to do what God has told you one minute; then make excuses as to why you can't do it the next. But just as the evil fairy couldn't kill or destroy Sleeping Beauty, Satan cannot destroy you.

That Sneaky Devil

Genesis 2:21-25 tells the story of the marriage institution, which was established with Adam and Eve. Chapter 3 shows that the devil was right there tempting Eve from the start. Verse 1 says, "Now the serpent was more subtle than any beast." *Webster's Dictionary* defines *subtle* as "so slight as to be difficult to detect or analyze (elusive): skillful or ingenious (clever):

51

marked by craft or slyness (devious): and/or operating in a hidden and usually injurious way (insidious)." That is how the devil works. In verse 5, Satan tempted Adam and Eve by saying, "For God knows that when you eat of it [the forbidden fruit] your eyes will be opened, and you will be like God, knowing good and evil" (NIV). Guess what? Adam and Eve were already like God because God had made them in His own image and likeness. The devil is subtle in that he tricks us into believing something just a little different from what is already true.

He will trick you into believing that your spouse is against you when he or she is not. For example, before you go to bed, your husband asks you to wake him up at 6:30 AM because he must attend a very important meeting at 8:00 AM. You get up at about 6:00 AM and start your day. At 7:00 AM, your husband comes to you angry because you didn't wake him up when you were supposed to. If he has the heart of his spouse, he will know that you would never do anything intentionally to hurt him. If you say that it completely slipped your mind or that you forgot, he should take that in stride.

Your spouse is not your enemy. The devil is, and he is using that situation to start an argument. Division is Satan's purpose because he wants to rule your household. The devil makes you think that your spouse is against you and doesn't want good things for you, but in reality, you would never have married a person who didn't want to do you good all the days of your life.

Know your authority in Christ. If you are a parent, would you let your kids run over you or tell you what to do? No! Then why, as a child of God who has authority over the devil, would you let him run your household? Slap him with the Word of God and rebuke him in Jesus' name and send him packing. I do it daily so that I don't give him rule even for one day. Luke 4:13 says, "And when the devil had ended all the temptation, he departed from [Jesus] for a season." The Word never says the devil won't come back. Daily I slap him with my restraining order (the Word of God) so that he and his demons must stay away from me, my family, and my property.

Jesus was tempted by the devil before He began His ministry. In fact, the devil used the Word of God to tempt Jesus. This tells us that we must know the Word. It seems as though before we got married, everything was fine. There were imperfections, but we loved that person anyway. Once we got married, all hell broke loose. Well, it is good to see that the devil is consistent! He shows up when God's plan is about to be made manifest. After Jesus was baptized, the devil came immediately to tempt Him (Luke 4:2). The difference between Christ and us is that He had more Word and was able to rebuke Satan because of His authority. But guess what? He has given us the same authority.

Every day, if you submit your life to God and resist and bind the works of the devil, he will flee from you (James 4:7). Know that Satan is after your marriage. As a married couple, the love of God is magnified because people should see God through your witness, your loving union. Please note that witnessing is not talking; it is how you live. It is what you do daily without even thinking about it. (We will discuss more about witnessing in Chapter 8.) The devil comes immediately to take the Word. His purpose is to kill, steal, and destroy (John 10:10). That includes you, your marriage, and anything that has to do with God. In a majority of the cases, the devil didn't mess with you before you got married because you were in sin— perhaps you were living with one another, having premarital sex, were not born again, and so on.

Trials and Tribulations

> Blessed (happy, to be envied) is the man who is patient under trial and stands up under temptation, for when he has stood the test and been approved, he will receive [the victor's] crown of life which God has promised to those who love Him. Let no one say when he is tempted, I am tempted from God; for God is incapable of being tempted by [what is] evil and He Himself tempts no one. (James 1:12-13 AB)

In this passage, God is saying that you will be tried and tested, and the devil will tempt you, but this tempting is not of God. What is of God is that you go through and pass the test so that your Father can give you all that He promises. God is a giving God; He only wants to give you His best.

First Peter 5:8-10 (AB) states:

Be well balanced (temperate, sober of mind), be vigilant and cautious at all times; for that enemy of yours, the devil [note: *not your husband or wife*—my addition] roams around like a lion roaring [in fierce hunger], seeking someone to seize upon and devour. Withstand him; be firm in faith [against his onset—rooted, established, strong, immovable, and determined], knowing that the same (identical) sufferings are appointed to your brotherhood (the whole body of Christians) throughout the world. And after you have suffered a little while, the God of all grace [Who imparts all blessing and favor], Who has called you to His [own] eternal glory in Christ Jesus, will Himself complete and make you what you ought to be, establish and ground you securely, and strengthen, and settle you. (AB)

That passage is so strong. God is saying that you are not the only one going through hard times in your marriage. So many Christian homes are being ruined because they don't know how to stay rooted, strong, and immovable when they are going through difficulty. This passage also blessed me because God says that, after a little while, He will take over and complete you and strengthen you—not your spouse. He is talking to the one who reads it.

When Lewis and I were separated, I asked God for answers, and He directed all revelation and answers toward me. He told me that I needed to change and that I needed to do this, that, and the other. When I asked about Lewis, He told me not to worry about him; that was His job. As you can see, I had to start the process, but God will finish it. God is now completing the rest.

When trials and tribulations come, just remember that it is only a test. It is not a time to run scared and be defeated, but to look at the situation as an opportunity for growth and maturity in faith. Paul reminds us of this in his letter to the Romans:

> Therefore, being justified by faith, we have peace with God through our Lord Jesus Christ, by whom also we have access by faith into this grace in which we stand, and rejoice in hope of the glory of God. And not only so, but we glory in tribulations also, knowing that tribulation worketh patience; and patience, experience; and experience, hope; and hope maketh not ashamed, because the love of God is shed abroad in our hearts by the Holy Ghost who is given unto us. (Romans 5:1-5)

Verse 5 in the Amplified says that, "such hope never disappoints or deludes or shames us, for God's love has been poured out in our hearts through the

Holy Spirit Who has been given to us." How can it be, as Christians, that when we are going through trial times, we feel no love for our spouses? You may think of it as "I love him, but I don't like him . . . He/she gets on my nerves . . . I don't like the things he/she does." As Christians, we have the Holy Spirit inside of us, and He produces only the fruit of love, joy, peace, patience, kindness, goodness, faithfulness, meekness, and self-control (Galatians 5:22-23). I realized that I didn't have to work on accomplishing those fruits because they were already in me. So when you're challenged in your marriage, go inside, because greater is He that lives on the inside of us than he [me — *my addition*] that is in the world (1 John 4:4).

Suffering

As I was crying out to the Lord, asking Him what happened in my marriage, God said: "Why do you call me, 'Lord, Lord,' and do not do the things I say?" (Luke 6:46). God said that I was denying Him because I denied His Word. I am going to the best Bible teaching church regularly, I read the Word of God on my own time, I watch Christian television often, I give tithes and offerings. So why was I calling on Him when I already knew the right things to do? They're in His Word.

God said, in most cases, that I was doing the Word but I wasn't killing my flesh. And because I was growing spiritually, my flesh and spirit were at odds with one another. I was walking in the Spirit one minute and walking in the flesh the next. Which really means that I was walking with God while holding the devil's hand. The devil was the ruler over my marriage because I was still in the flesh when it came to dealing with my husband and our marital issues.

Whenever you are being delivered, set free, and moving towards the things of God, your flesh is going to wrestle with your spirit. "For our struggle is not against flesh and blood, but against the rulers, against the authorities, against the powers of this dark world and against the spiritual forces of evil in the heavenly realms"—Satan himself (Ephesians 6:12 NIV). When we are arguing with our spouses, we know that Satan is behind the confusion, not our spouses. That is why there was warfare in my mind; the Holy Spirit was telling me to do the things of God, but the devil was trying to get me to do things his way. I was trying to make my marriage work based on how the world said it should work, and as my example, I was looking at those marriages that have influenced my life (divorced couples, TV, movies, novels, and so on).

If we don't do the things God tells us in His Word, Satan has just deceived us and we have given him control over our marriages. But know, once we start to grow up spiritually, he will step up to the plate to stop our growth. The good news is, God will only allow the devil to go so far. That's how we know we have the victory, because our Father controls and puts limits on what the devil can do (see Job 1:6-12). We cannot blame God for the struggles we go through. Instead, we need to look at the sin (acts of disobedience to God's Word). For example, if you're not tithing, this opens the door for sin. Therefore, the door is open to financial problems. Although God will finish the work, you must start the process: Repent and start tithing.

So the devil's focus was on how he could separate me, not only from my husband, but from the will of God for our lives. God gives us choices, life or death, but He urges us to choose life (Deuteronomy 30:19). With God, there is life; and with the devil, there is death. Since God through Jesus Christ has recovered all that the devil had stolen through Adam and Eve, Satan's purpose is to get as many Christians back under his rule as he can. He doesn't need sinners—those that don't know Christ—because he already has them. So when those thoughts come into your mind, saying, "It doesn't take all that to be a Christian. It's too hard to be a Christian. I will never be perfect. I am doing pretty good with my life the way it is," *you have just been deceived by the devil.* I used to fall prey to those thoughts; but because I know who I am in Jesus, I know that I can fall short sometimes, repent, and continue in the path of righteousness.

Baits

The devil will put ideas in your head—thoughts of adultery or jealous suspicion about someone who works with your mate. Cast out that evil spirit! Don't own the thought or let it stay in your mind. Cast down imaginations and every high thing that exalts itself against the knowledge of God and bring into captivity every thought to the obedience of Christ (2 Corinthians 10:5). For example, if the devil says, "Your husband doesn't love you," turn it around and say, "My husband loves me as Christ loves the church" (Ephesians 5:25). Or if the devil says, "You can't get out of the adulterous affair," then say, "I can do all things through Christ who strengthens me" (Philippians 4:13). Or if the devil whispers, "Your husband will never change," then reply, "With man it is impossible, but with God all things are possible" (Matthew 19:26). In order to defeat the devil, you *must* speak the Word of God. It is like stabbing him with a sword, which is a nickname for the Bible.

Here are some other weapons the devil uses to keep you in the flesh:

1. Lies you tell.
2. Mean-spirited words you speak.
3. Erroneous and exaggerated thoughts you think (i.e., "All my husband thinks about is sex").
4. Believing the voice of the devil, which is either opposite of the Word of God or twisted (i.e., the devil was in the garden with Eve and told her, "You shall not surely die," yet God told Adam they would surely die).

When you sense the devil attacking you, these are some things you should do:

1. Avoid sinning with your tongue (Psalm 39:1).

2. Pray and ask God what you should do (Proverbs 3:5-6).
3. Fast. It helps kill your flesh (Matthew 6:16-18).
4. Trust God during this time (Psalm 37:5).
5. Meditate on God's Word (Joshua 1:8).
6. Adhere to God's voice and do what He tells you to do (Luke 6:47-48).

Father, I thank You that You have given me authority to bind all things (the devil, evil spirits, anything not of You) that work against me and release Your power through Your Words. I thank You that Your Word is truth and I don't have to live a lie, that my marriage can and will be all that You have called it to be. Cast out all things (bitterness, hatred, anger, criticisms) that may irritate my spouse and cause me to stir up strife. Let Your love and kindness, Father, rule my life and control all that I say and do. Amen.

My tribulations brought me to the feet of Jesus. I had never been more desperate to hear from God and to see Him move in my life. I was totally ready to submit to all that He commanded in order to turn my life around. He told me that being totally submissive is a great start.

Chapter 4

The Bonfire

Submit to one another out of reverence for Christ. (Ephesians 5:21 NIV)

We all have someone of a higher authority to whom we must answer. As an employee, you submit to your supervisor. As Christians, we submit ourselves to the will of God. Even in the story of Sleeping Beauty, the townspeople submitted to the king's authority to get rid of all of their spinning wheels. Submission to one another is what we do unto God and out of reverence for God and His Word.

Submission

Submission is a new way of thinking for men and women. But first, we must stop thinking of the word *submission* as an ugly word and move away from the idea that it means to be ruled and dominated. The *Student Bible Dictionary* definition of *submission* and *submit* is "Yield. Christian submission is to voluntarily yield in love and consider another's needs more important than one's own." It is not an act; it is an attitude of the heart.

How do we submit to our men or women of God? Philippians 2:3-5 says,

Do nothing from factional motives [through contentiousness, strife, selfishness, or for unworthy ends] or prompted by conceit and empty arrogance. Instead, in the true spirit of humility (lowliness of mind) let each regard the others as better than and superior to himself [thinking more highly of one another than you do of yourselves]. Let each of you esteem and look upon and be concerned for not [merely] his own interests, but also each for the interests of others. Let this same attitude and purpose and [humble] mind be in you which was in Christ Jesus: [Let him be your example in humility]. (AB)

I believe this next verse talks of submission as supporting your husband's mission: "Wives, be subject (be submissive and adapt yourselves) to your own husbands as (a service) to the Lord" (Ephesians 5:22 AB). Submission simply means to humble yourself before God; not before man or woman, but God. Both men and women have a responsibility to put on the attitude of submitting to one another.

Again, your spouse is not your enemy. Think of submission as humbling yourself before God and not your mate. God's Word says to "submit yourselves to every ordinance of man *for the Lord's sake"(*1 Peter 2:13). Queen Vashti, in the book of Esther, decided she did not want to submit to the king when he requested her presence at his party. She looked at her husband's request in the wrong way. Because she was his glory, he wanted to show her off as the beautiful woman she was. However, she took it upon herself to see his request as an offense. She was probably thinking, "I am not going out there in front of all those drunken men." She looked at it as honoring her husband versus honoring God through submission.

Let's consider a personal example. Suppose that you and your husband are at a dinner party, and in the middle of the conversation, he asks you to get him something to drink. Do you say, "Who does he think I am? He should go get it himself," and actually make him get it? No, this is an opportunity to submit, honor your man of God, and witness to others of Christ in you. Humble yourself before God, not your mate. I have finally come to a place where I see being submissive as simply honoring my man of God. (Notice that I didn't say honoring Lewis. By saying "man of God," we may see them differently than just as mere men.)

Submission is not an act. It should be the very core of your being. For example, people may say that you are a touchy-feely person, and you say, "That is just who I am." Well, you don't act touchy-feely. That is just who you are. Just as witnessing (showing Jesus' love in you) is not an act. It's what people should see through you. God is trying to tell us to stop acting and become like Jesus. Just do what the Word says, and be more like Him. God doesn't have to act nice toward us—He just is. Because we are born again, we have the gift of the Holy Spirit, and He has all we need so that we don't have to act. We just have to be led by Him.

Division

First Corinthians 1:10 states, "Now I beseech you, brethren, by the name of our Lord Jesus Christ, that ye all speak the same thing, and that there be no divisions among you, but that ye be perfectly joined together in the same mind and in the same judgment." One thing that causes division in a marriage is the wife trying to go ahead of her husband. Remember, "If a house be divided against itself, that house cannot stand" (Mark 3:25). Eve let the devil influence her and caused humanity to separate from God. God drove out Adam, and Adam's relationship with God changed forever. Division causes a change for the worse. Division is caused by being led by your flesh.

If Eve had been a stronger wife, the devil's influence would not have divided her house because she would have had the heart of her man of God. She could have easily purposed in her heart not to eat the fruit because her husband told her not to. That would have been submission. I am not blaming her for the fall of man, because ultimately it was Adam's responsibility to say no, since he was the head. But women of God, we have to make sure that we are submitted to our husbands to help them do what God has told them to do.

Who (or what) are you going to let divide your household? Your single friends, your unbelieving family members, your own expectations as to what you think something or someone should be? Our mates are who God has made them to be. Who are you to change them or even want them to change? When you start wanting to change someone else, always look inside yourself first. Ask yourself what *you* need to change about your circumstances or situation. God will always tell you about you.

Romans 2:1 (NIV) says, "You, therefore, have no excuse, you who pass judgment on someone else, for at whatever point you judge the other, you are condemning yourself, because you who pass judgment do the same things." No matter what we think, we all fall into the trap of judging, and it's deadly in a marriage. My husband and I were saved before we got married, but Lewis didn't go to church often.

I would wake up on Sunday mornings and start nagging.

"Are you going to church this morning?"

"No," he would answer.

I would come back with, "Oh, you could go out last night, but you can't get up and go to church. If it were a business meeting, you would get up in a minute!"

That's judging. God showed me that I needed to mind my own business. Your spouse is not your business; he or she is God's business, and God does not need little gods helping Him do His job.

Also, don't let the devil deceive you into thinking that you are better than your mate. You are equals; that is why you can submit to one another. However, women, no matter where you are spiritually, God will not elevate you above your head. I've been saved and serving God much longer than Lewis. I go to church faithfully, and I am active. In my flesh, I may think I am more spiritual than he is. However, I am not. God could cause my head to rise above me at any time; and as long as I am submissive, there will be no clashes. So, if you are totally submissive to your man of God, as you increase in the things of God, so will he. My husband has grown spiritually because I have, and he probably doesn't even realize how far he has come. In just one year, Lewis goes to church more, he tithes, he prays and reads the Word more, and he even went to a Men's conference. This is big! Whatever the call of the Lord is on your spouse's life, if you submit, you help him or her to become all he or she should be.

United in Spirit

God will speak to your man of God as well as to you. He is the Father of order and decency. He told Mary that she would be pregnant with a child not of Joseph, but He told Joseph before she did. He also continued speaking to Joseph instead of Mary concerning what Joseph should do regarding his family. She just had to follow her man of God.

When you get married, pray continually that your spirits always line up with one another. God will not withhold any good thing from you. "Can two walk together, except they be agreed?" (Amos 3:3).

To be united in spirit with our spouses is being agreeable, sympathetic, compassionate, and humble. Our goal should be living to please our spouses, to esteem them more highly than ourselves (Philippians 2:3). I ask the Holy Spirit daily about what I should do concerning Lewis, the children, and our family business. I ask God to speak to him and to me so that we can be in agreement about all things.

God is no respecter of persons. Just as He sent angels to speak to Abraham and Sarah about the name of their son Isaac, He can speak to you daily concerning what you need to know about one another.

Here are some ways to help you and your mate become closer:

1. Ask your mate to tell you one thing you can do for him or her this week (nothing sexual).
2. Make one day a month or even a week of pleasing, doing anything and everything that will please your mate (don't tell him or her what you are going to do or when you're going to do it).
3. Pray for God to reveal something about your mate that day, listen to the Lord's voice, and do it (for example, your spouse may be thinking, "It sure would be nice to have lunch at my favorite restaurant," and God may tell you to call him or her for a lunch date).
4. Give your spouse the day off (men cook and take care of the kids that evening, or women let their husbands come home and rest with dinner in bed).

5   Acknowledge them and praise them daily
    for the little things.
6. Always look at one another through
    spiritual eyes.

As Peter advises:

In the same way you married men
should live considerately with [your
wives], with an intelligent recognition
[of the marriage relation], honoring the
woman as [physically] the weaker, but
[realizing that you] are joint heirs of the
grace (God's unmerited favor) of life, in
order that your prayers may not be
hindered and cut off. [Otherwise, you
cannot pray effectively.] Finally, all [of
you] should be of one and the same
mind (united in spirit), sympathizing
[with one another], loving [each other]
as brethren [of one household],
compassionate and courteous
(tenderhearted and humble). (1 Peter
3:7-8 AB)

As Peter stated, we are joint heirs of grace. Men
must honor their wives, or as the Word states, their
prayers will be hindered. Being of the same mind is
simply submitting yourselves one to another in love for
the sake of Christ. Look at Jesus' attitude regarding
submission. In Luke 22:42, when the time had come
for Him to fulfill God's purpose, He prays, "Father, if

thou be willing, remove this cup from me: nevertheless not my will, but thine, be done." Look at His heart: I don't want to, Father, but *nevertheless*, I will because you want Me to.

> Pray daily, *"Father, I ask that my spirit will always line up with _____ (your spouse) and that every time You speak to him/her about something, You will speak to me as well, so that we can totally be in one accord. In the name of Jesus, Amen.*

Chapter 5

Prick Your Finger

I beseech [beg] you therefore, brethren, by the mercies of God, that ye present your bodies a living sacrifice, holy, acceptable unto God, which is your reasonable service. And be not conformed to this world, but be ye transformed by the renewing of your mind, that ye may prove what is that good, and acceptable, and perfect will of God. (Romans 12:1-2)

Just pause and think about that Scripture. What does it mean to you? God wants us to die to our flesh so that we may do all He's called us to do, which is our reasonable service. Sleeping Beauty pricked her finger on the spinning wheel; yet though she was thought to be dead, she was still alive. Dying to our flesh, yet though we live, we die. Although it may be a somewhat painful experience, it really is just a decision you make to do God's will. It is as simple as pricking your finger. Although it may hurt for a moment, it doesn't kill you.

Denying Self

After Lewis and I separated and I was desperately seeking God for answers, He told me to go to John 19:18, which reads, "Where they crucified him, and two others with him, on either side one, and Jesus in the midst."

I knew that two robbers died with Jesus, but God said, "No, look at them as sinners. Put your husband on one side and you on the other."

I said, "Okay, now what?"

He said, "Die."

How do we do that? By doing everything opposite of what our flesh tells us. For example, if Lewis asks me to cook and I don't want to, but I do anyway; that brings me closer to the cross. Or when we are arguing and the Holy Spirit tells us to shut up, and we do it; that brings us closer to the cross. Or if I am acting foolishly and the Holy Spirit tells Lewis to bless me, and he does; it brings him closer to the cross. By the time both husband and wife die to self, they will be centered with Jesus in the midst, and the two shall become one. As Paul urges us, "Then make my joy complete by being like-minded, having the same love, being one in spirit and purpose" (Philippians 2:2 NIV).

Do you remember what Jesus told us about dying to ourselves?

> If any person wills to come after Me, let him deny himself [disown himself, forget, lose sight of himself and his own

interests, refuse and give up himself]
and take up his cross daily and follow
Me [cleave steadfastly to Me, conform
wholly to My example in living and, if
need be, in dying, also]. (Luke 9:23
AB)

Daily means that it is a continuing process. Your
flesh is never dead until you die a physical death, so
you must work on killing its desires every day.

No, you don't physically kill yourself. It is a
fleshly death whereby your spirit comes alive. You kill
what you want, what you feel, and what you think
when it is contrary to God's will. Before Jesus died,
He prayed for God to remove the cup; yet He wanted
not His will but God's will to be done. It was never
about what Jesus wanted, what He felt, or what He
thought. He wanted to do what was right in the sight of
God. When you die to your flesh, you accept the cup
(all the things your spouse does that you don't like and
all the things your spouse asks you to do that you don't
want to do), allowing God's will, not your will, to be
done in your marriage.

Here are some examples:

1. Killing what I think.
   • If God tells the husband to have his wife
     quit her job and stay at home to raise
     their children, just do it. Trust God, His
     grace is sufficient.

- Die to your pet peeves. (So what if he doesn't seal the bag in the cereal box? You do it.)

2. Killing what I want.
   - Die to sin: smoking, drinking, drugs, sex outside of marriage.
   - Die to your plans, goals, and aspirations, and seek God's plans for your life.

3. Killing what I feel.
   - If your husband wants you to cook every night, cook.
   - Help and give to others, even when you think you don't have the time.

It takes just one person in the marriage to stay in the Word and work towards a heavenly marriage for it to stay somewhat peaceful. Why? Because when one is in the flesh and the other remains in the Spirit, both aren't acting like fools. The one being led by the Holy Spirit can bring stability, encouragement, and growth to the relationship, because that partner is continuing to grow spiritually—he or she is building the inner man. Praying, praise and worship, reading the Word, and fellowshipping with God will help to build your inner man. As you continue to grow, it becomes much easier to die to what you think, feel, and want. As Paul wrote, "I am crucified with Christ: nevertheless I live; yet not I, but Christ liveth in me: and the life which I now live in the flesh I live by the faith of the Son of God, who loved me, and gave himself for me" (Galatians 2:20).

Our marriages are to be patterned after Christ's love for the church. In 1 John 3:16, it says, "Hereby perceive we the love of God, because he laid down his life for us: and we ought to lay down our lives for the brethren." Because of Jesus' love for the church, He gave of Himself (died); and because He was resurrected, we, too, can die so that our lives and marriages can live again. Why is it that we can die to our ways when we have children or get a job, but we have trouble when it comes to our spouse? When you have a baby, you die to your flesh because it's all about the baby's needs and not yours. When the baby awakes at midnight, 3 AM, and 6 AM, you must get up. When you get a job, you die to what you want and you do what is necessary to keep that job. Some of us have to get up at 4 AM just to get to work on time. But the very gift (husband or wife) God has given us, we are selfish with and we cannot die for.

In John 21:15-17 (NIV), Jesus asked Peter three times if he loved Him. Peter got angry at first and then said, "Jesus, you know all things. Yes, I love you." Then, in verse 18-19, Jesus said, "I tell you the truth, when you were younger you dressed yourself and went where you wanted; but when you are old you will stretch out your hands, and someone else will dress you and lead you where you do not want to go. Jesus said this to indicate the kind of death by which Peter would glorify God." Then He said to Peter, "Follow me." In order to follow Jesus and glorify God, we must die.

Grace

God gives us sufficient grace to do the work of the ministry He has given us. He knew what He was doing when He put you and your spouse together. When your friend says, "If he were my husband, I wouldn't take that," it's because there's no grace for her concerning that man. But there is grace for you when dealing with your husband; that's why he's *your* husband. That is also why you can't let people talk you out of what God has in store for you and your spouse. In the book of Esther, King Ahasuerus let his officers (wise men) talk him into divorce over Queen Vashti's disobedience. They fed him thoughts ("What would happen to us if our wives knew what she did? They wouldn't respect us either."). They told the king why he couldn't let Queen Vashti get away with it. In Esther 2:1, we read that when he cooled down, "He began brooding over the loss of Vashti, realizing that he would never see her again" (TLB). His hasty decision and the counsel of others led him to a place of divorce, where he never wanted to be.

There is a grace for the husband to be the head and for a wife to be a helpmeet. Struggles come when you work outside your grace, but there is peace and rest when you work within the grace you've been given. When you stop working on the problems in your marriage, there is a grace that comes to you. "And if by grace, then is it no more of works; otherwise, grace is no more grace [God's favor]" (Romans 11:6 AB). When you are weak and can't seem to go on, factor in the grace that God gives you.

Honoring God

We honor God when we honor our man or woman of God. There was a time when Lewis and I were arguing over me fixing dinner. I told him I would not fix him dinner, and he told me I'd *better*. I was so mad, and we were arguing at the top of our voices, and he walked out. The first thing that came to my mind was, "Wait until he comes home! I will have bread and water waiting for him." The second thought that came was from God.

"Will you honor man or Me?"

I said, "You, God."

He said, "Now call your man of God, apologize, and ask him what he wants for dinner." I did just that, and then God said, "What you do unto Lewis you do unto Me. You honor Me through honoring him."

Remember this Scripture? "Serve wholeheartedly, as if you were serving the Lord, not men" (Ephesians 6:7 NIV). I then asked God what had happened; how did Lewis and I even go there. The Holy Spirit revealed to me that Lewis doesn't like leftovers. That is why he doesn't put food up in the evening.

We need to get out of fleshly thinking: "He doesn't tell *me* what to do" . . . "Who does she think I am" . . . "I am my own person." We need to renew our minds. We need to start thinking about how we can honor God through our man/woman of God. This also applies to disagreements with friends, coworkers, parents, and so on. By apologizing and doing what is right in the sight of God, you honor God. It should be easier for us to do when we realize that we aren't bowing to that person, but to God. We have to get rid of the stinking thinking that says if we do what's right, we are giving in to them, even when they are wrong. As Christians, we are to honor God, and when we honor Him above our own feelings, it is the love of God in us that can love people at all times. Ministry starts with love. That is one reason you get married—because of the love you have for one another. Next, we'll look at the marriage ministry.

> *Father, thank You for the Word, the truth—that I may be set free to do Your will. I present my body to You as a living sacrifice that I may walk in the Spirit, talk in the Spirit, and live in the Spirit. Father, not my will, but Your will be done from this day forward. Now, in the name of Jesus, I decree and declare that my flesh is no longer on the throne and my spirit is quickened and I am changed. In Jesus' name, Amen.*

Chapter 6
Deep Sleep

And the Lord God caused a deep sleep to fall upon Adam, and he slept: and he took one of his ribs, and closed up the flesh instead thereof. And the rib, which the Lord God had taken from man, made he a woman, and brought her unto the man. And Adam said, This is now bone of my bones, and flesh of my flesh: she shall be called Woman, because she was taken out of Man. Therefore shall a man leave his father and his mother, and shall cleave unto his wife: and they shall be one flesh. (Genesis 2:21-24)

That scripture is the start of the marriage ministry. Yet, right afterwards, Adam and Eve sinned and were sent forth from the Garden of Eden. God's perfect plan for their lives was destroyed, and they were now in darkness. Sleeping Beauty was in darkness until her Prince Charming came. For years, Lewis and I had no clue (vision) as to God's plan or purpose for our marriage; therefore, we were in complete darkness for several years. When we go into our marriages, we should know His plan and purpose and walk in it. For others who are married and don't know God's plan for their lives, it is time to seek the Lord. Each couple's ministry begins with their marriage.

About My Father's Business

Marriage is an institution God created and is glorified in because two individuals can witness His love on the earth. Just as the Father, Son, and Holy Spirit are one, a trinity is established in your marriage as well: you, your spouse, and Jesus. Unfortunately, the one we often leave out of our marriages is Jesus. Before Jesus started His ministry, I believe between the ages of 12 and 30, He was studying the Word, developing a relationship with His Father, and seeking God's plan and purpose for His life. Jesus didn't do anything that His Father didn't tell Him to do, nor did He do anything of Himself. Yet we think we can get married and work out the marriage and its issues by ourselves. God says we don't have to because He is with us always. If we are truly a part of the marriage trinity, everything we do and say should be what the Father tells us.

This is not difficult if we are led by the Holy Spirit and not our flesh. God is a God of simplicity. It is very easy to copy Christ. For thirty years, Jesus developed a relationship with His Father. As a young boy, He told His parents, "How is it that you had to look for Me? Did you not see and know that it is necessary [as a duty] for Me to be in My Father's house and [occupied] about My Father's business?" (Luke 2:49 AB). It is time for our marriages to be about our Father's business.

Christian men and women of God should not be getting divorces. How can we call ourselves Christians and be like the world? As Christians, we are to show God on earth; we are to show that His way is perfect. Christianity is not a title, a religion, or what we do. It's who we are. It says that you are a woman or man after God's own heart, that you don't just go to church to hear the Word, but you do the Word that you hear (James 1:22). God is looking for us to fulfill His will. This Christian walk is not about you or me. It is about doing our Father's business. God wants all the people on earth to be reconciled to Him and out of the hands of Satan. As Christians, we are to witness God's love so that lost souls can be reconciled back to Him. God is a God of purpose; therefore, your marriage has a purpose.

Religion Versus Relationship

When I was growing, up, all I knew about having a relationship with God was going to church every Sunday. Reading the Bible, praying, and entering into God's presence in my very home was not a reality. My thought was I had one day a year, my birthday, to ask God for something I really wanted. Now I know that going to church is not enough. Going to Bible study is not enough. We must, in our quiet time, seek His face and His will for our lives. When Lewis and I separated, my first thought was that I needed to call the church for counseling. Then I thought, "There is only one person who knows all and can tell me exactly what I need to do. And that is God." So I sought His face. I entered into His presence with praise and worship. I got into a quiet place where I asked questions and opened my ears to hear from Him. I read the Word more, and I let it convict my heart. And I began to change.

Equally Yoked

All marriages have a purpose. For example, my pastors were brought together to preach the Word of God. I see God through them. Know that God brings equals together, which means that both individuals bring something to the marriage that God can use in a mighty way. He takes the strength of one to cover the weaknesses of another. That is why both are to submit one to another; one who is weak in one area should submit to the other who is strong in that area. That is why you should not look at or talk about the weaknesses of your mate. Your strength covers that person's weaknesses, and that is how you can elevate them. You might have thought that meeting your spouse was just coincidental—something about them pleased you. I don't think so. Nothing just happens. God knew when, who, why, and how you were going to come together. Again, it's not about you; it's about your Father's business.

If you are not married yet, find that common denominator between the two of you. Ask yourself, How could God use us? In 2 Corinthians 6:14, Paul says, "Do not be unequally yoked with unbelievers [do not make mismatched alliances with them or come under a different yoke with them, inconsistent with your faith]" (AB). For the most part, this talks about believers and nonbelievers. For example, a Christian marrying a Muslim is not right. But it also means that both individuals should be equal in other things as well.

For example, a woman who loves to wear mink coats should not be married to an animal activist. They are unequally yoked. For some of us, it may mean that we need to stop hanging out with single friends, especially those who are of the wrong influence. God is a God of order and decency, and He always puts equals together. Now the couple who has an interest in animals should be together, and that is how God can use your marriage as a ministry. If you look at most successful couples, they have something in common. Look at pastors. The majority of the time, if he has been called into the ministry, she has too. As another example, my husband and I both have entrepreneurial minds. Ever since I was in elementary school, I have wanted to own my own business. When Lewis and I met, he stated that his desire was to have a business too. I never thought about it at first, but that is one of the reasons why God put us together—to have a business ministry.

When we separated and I was seeking God for answers, He said that my marriage was out of order. My thought was that Transparent Communications Network (TCN) was Lewis' business, his vision, and I had to get my own. But God told me no, it was His vision and I was called to be a helpmeet for God's business. That was one reason Lewis and I were together. I was trying to start a business at the same time TCN was taking off, and Lewis really needed my help. God now has us ministering to high school students who might want to start a business.

We are living epistles for Christ. Those children and others should see Christ in us. So our marriage is not just a marriage; it is a ministry in which people can learn about Christ without us opening the Bible or giving Scripture verses. That is why it is important to be equally yoked in mind, body, and spirit.

This is not to say that couples can't have two businesses, but one may have to be put on hold for a while. God needs us (Christians) to have businesses for Him. But everything must be done in decency and order. For example, former President Clinton and First Lady Hillary were equally yoked in that they both loved politics. However, if she had gone after her dreams at the time her husband was President, that would have caused much division in their home as well as in the country. She waited until she helped him do his part, then she did hers. Although I do not know them personally or what, if any, faith they hold, God showed me Him through them. In public, she stood by her man at a very difficult and embarrassing time. She never talked bad about him, she covered his weaknesses with her strength, and she respected her husband even when public opinion thought she shouldn't have. Look at how God can use people. I believe she is what God would call a virtuous woman.

How can you be a helpmeet if you don't know or experience what your husband does? That is why you see so many husband-and-wife teams in the ministry today. God put those two individuals together because they are equally yoked in their calling. Eve was created so she could help Adam tend the garden. Most successful couples work in the same career field, enjoy the same type of activitics (photography, mountain climbing, etc.) or have the same interests (helping homeless people, animal activism, etc.).

What do you and your mate have in common? If you don't know, ask your spouse about his or her dreams and interests. Above all, ask God what His plans and purposes are for your marriage.

In order to fulfill your purpose, you must develop a relationship with your Heavenly Father. Just as you talk to those whom you desire to know, talk to Him every day and ask questions. Trust me, He will answer every one of them. You can start by asking, "Is my home (family) a place where God dwells?" God wants to hear from you about every aspect of your life. He wants to lead you to the good life and down the right path. Find your common ground. I assure you that when you do, and when you start working together, your marriage will become all God has called it to be.

The Bible tells us of a couple, Priscilla and Aquila, whose purpose was to establish churches. They both were tentmakers (equally yoked) who opened their home as a meeting place. Both were well versed in the Word of God and helped people understand it. If you read their story in Acts 18, it is short and sweet, but God wants you to see that everyone has a purpose. It may not be mighty in deed, but God was pleased with what they did. Will you be faithful in your ministry at home? Do you show the love of Jesus to your spouse and children? Or do they just see it on Sundays at church? Your family is your first ministry. Once you are successful in that, God will move you to do other things.

Christ, the Foundation

According to my Bible, God's plan for marriage is for one man and one woman to marry for a lifetime. A mutually supportive attitude must characterize both the husband and wife if they are to succeed in building a harmonious home. Why are some marriages hell on earth? Because we are trying to fight our own battles. We don't have enough of the Word in us. We lack knowledge when it comes to marriage. We want to be Christians, in that we are active in the church and praising God around other believers, but we want to act like people of the world when it comes to our marriages and home life. We never separate the world's way of marriage from God's way. As I said before, His way is perfect. And His foundation is sure and strong.

> For we are fellow workmen (joint promoters, laborers together) with and for God; [you are] God's garden and vineyard and field under cultivation, you are God's building. According to the grace (the special endowment for my task) of God bestowed on me, like a skillful architect and master builder I laid [the] foundation, and now another [man] is building upon it. But let each

[man] be careful how he builds upon it, for no other foundation can anyone lay than that which is [already] laid, which is Jesus Christ (the Messiah, the Anointed One). But if anyone builds upon the Foundation, whether it be with gold, silver, precious stones, wood, hay, straw, the work of each [one] will become [plainly, openly] known (shown for what it is); for the day [of Christ] will disclose and declare it, because it will be revealed with fire, and the fire will test and critically appraise the character and worth of the work each person has done. If the work which any person has built on this Foundation [any product of his efforts whatever] survives [this test], he will get his reward. But if any person's work is burned up [under the test], he will suffer the loss [of it all, losing his reward], though he himself will be saved, but only as [one who has passed] through fire. (1 Corinthians 3:9-15 AB)

If you build your home on any other foundation than Christ, the house will fall when the storms come. This is why there are so many divorces, even within the church. Like Lewis and me, even though we were both saved, many Christians do not build the foundation of their marriage completely on the Word of God. Therefore, the cracks that inevitably appear in the foundation are widened further by the devil.

So what do you do? Reestablish the house (your family) on the strong foundation of Christ, which means reading and doing all that the Word tells you to do. As it says in Proverbs, "Through skillful and godly Wisdom is a house (a life, a home, a family) built, and by understanding it is established [on a sound and good foundation], and by knowledge shall its chambers [of every area] be filled with all precious and pleasant riches" (24:3-4 AB).

> *Father, I pray that You would look upon me and my spouse and seal our marriage with Your love. We want to be about Your business, and we want to walk in the destiny You have planned for us. Lord, help us to change and grow so that we may prove what is Your good and acceptable and perfect will for our lives. In Jesus' name, Amen.*

Chapter 7

The Awakening

Awake thou that sleepest, and arise from the dead, and Christ shall give thee light. (Ephesians 5:14)

Prince Charming kissed Sleeping Beauty and she awoke with a smile on her face and love in her heart. At a Marriage Conference, I was awakened to the fact that I was a wife out of position and out of control. My thoughts, my actions, and my words were not in line with the Word of God. I was walking with God and holding the devil's hand, which meant that I was still in my flesh concerning my marriage. God dealt with me about the following: (1) order regarding my family, (2) sex in my marriage, (3) excuses for not doing what I knew was right, and (4) actions and words I was sowing into my marriage.

Decency and Order

The Apostle Paul gave the Corinthian church some instructions that reveal the nature of God: "God is not the author of confusion but of peace . . . [so] let all things be done decently and in order" (1 Corinthians 14:33, 40). What goes for the church also goes for individual Christians and our marriages, and there's an order that we should follow to avoid confusion and promote peace in our families.

That order is as follows:

1. God
2. Jesus
3. Man
4. Woman
5. Children
6. Ministry (church activities)

When you get married, the two of you become one flesh. You cleave to your spouse. Then, when you have children, you produce a godly seed. But notice, God never says in His Word to cleave to your children. They are God's responsibility (He ultimately is their provider through you), and your job is to love them and train them in the way they should go (Proverbs 22:6). Ephesians 6:4 also says, "Fathers, provoke not your children to wrath: but bring them up in the nurture and admonition of the Lord." Those children are not yours. God is just using you as a vessel to bring them into the world and raise them to be men and women of God. Jesus wasn't Mary's to hold onto either. Her job was just to love and train Him.

All this is to say that, women, you cannot put your children before your husband. That is out of order. Just as you would never put your husband before God, so you must not put your kids before your man of God. Now some of you might be saying, "I have to take care of my kids. They can't take care of themselves," or

"They are blood and he's not," or "He could leave one day, but my kids will always be with me." I used to say the same things, and God had to work with me. If you rationalize that your husband could leave or that his blood doesn't run through your veins, you have not entered into the type of marriage God has ordained. Your husband is bone to bone and flesh to flesh; you two have become one, which is closer than anything on this earth, including a child.

Just think, God says "cleave" to your spouse. *Cleave* in the Greek is *kollao*, which comes from the Greek word *kolla*, which means "glue." If you glue anything together, wallpaper to a wall, paper to paper, and try to tear it from one another, you'll get a piece left on the other. You cannot completely tear something apart that is glued together. That is how God intended marriage to be. You cannot completely separate from your husband. There is always a part of him with you. However, God says that a man (your son) should *leave* (not cleave to) his mother and father (Matthew 19:5). God says that children will leave and should separate themselves from their parents. That son then cleaves to his wife, and he and his wife become one. With the new couple, God starts another church/family (a place where God dwells).

Please understand that the husband and wife are lifetime partners. They build a foundation before the children come. When the children arrive, the couple has about eighteen years to train them, and then they move into adulthood to start their own families. During this time, the couple must maintain a level of commitment towards one another. They cannot allow the children to shift their focus so that they lose sight of one another. Remember, your children are going to leave. You and your spouse are still a church when they are gone. Is your house in order?

I made the mistake of putting ministry before my family. I would go to church meetings and wouldn't fix dinner. So my husband would come home after working all day to no meal. Yes, his hands worked just fine and he could have fixed his own meal, but per our agreement, cooking dinner was my responsibility. Instead, on Bible study nights, I would stop at a fast-food restaurant and the kids would eat on their way to church. That is wrong! I was so concerned about what I needed to do for the church, and what I thought God wanted me to do for the church, that I wasn't actually doing what was pleasing to Him. I wasn't taking care of my number-one ministry: the family He gave me. We have to find a balance in all we do without jeopardizing our families.

Sex in Marriage

In 1 Corinthians, Paul gives this advice regarding marital relations: "Do not deprive each other except by mutual consent and for a time, so that you may devote yourselves to prayer. Then come together again so that Satan will not tempt you because of your lack of self-control" (7:5 NIV). Sex is a vital, God-given part of your marriage. Instead of thinking of it as an act or even calling it "sex," think of it as you and your husband ministering to one another.

Why do we have problems in our marriages regarding sex? The answer is selfishness. We don't consider the other's needs. We only do it when we are interested. Lewis and I had to find a balance because I am a morning person and he is an evening person. We had to talk about it and make a commitment to meet one another's needs, even if that meant compromising on exactly what each of us wants for ourselves. It really boils down to this: Is your marriage worth keeping, or would you rather not compromise and risk your spouse having an affair to get his or her needs met?

If you are having sex only once a month or less, you may have a problem in your marriage (unless there are health needs, physical or emotional problems that prohibit it, or this is the frequency you and your spouse are comfortable with). A lack of intimacy can be a door for sin to enter and destroy your marriage, especially if one of you is feeling consistently frustrated, lonely, or unloved. So communicate with your spouse about your needs and desires. And remember to show your affection. Kiss your spouse. Don't just give a quick, thoughtless peck as you're on your way out the door, but take time to mean it, and put a little passion in your kisses. Take delight in your spouse and in your love for each other, as Solomon and his bride did in the Song of Solomon: "Let him kiss me with the kisses of his mouth. For thy love is better than wine" (1:2).

Excuses Are Not Acceptable

The third area of my marriage in which the Lord awoke me concerned my disrespect for Lewis. I did not do this intentionally. I didn't realize that I was not honoring my man of God as I should have. Even though Lewis, according to my standards, wasn't doing what he should have been doing spiritually, this gave me no excuse to look at him other than as the head of my marriage and family. Because I was the one who was growing spiritually, it was even more my responsibility to submit to the Word of God by submitting to my husband. Still, I questioned how he could lead me, especially in the things of God, if he wasn't even going to church.

Lewis was born again when we met and was very involved in church, but when his mom passed away, he became angry with God. Sadly, my failure to submit didn't bring him any closer to the Lord. He couldn't see God's love in anything, and even though I was going to church, my witness was hypocritical. Instead of loving him and showing him compassion and tenderness, I condemned him for not being where I was, for not being where he should be, and for not being a godly father in raising his girls.

The Lord finally told me to leave Lewis alone and concentrate on Him. So I kept my mouth shut, continued doing things in the church, enrolled in ministerial school, and did everything God told me to do (which are the things talked about in this book). It is now a little over one year since we reconciled, and things are so much better.

Lewis came downstairs one night when I was reading the Bible and asked, "Baby, can we do Bible study together?"

I said, "Yes, why?"

He said, "I want what you have, the Word of God in me."

Hallelujah! As I stated before, Lewis is hungry for the Lord. He is reading the Word. We pray together more, and he goes to church much more. Look how God can move on your behalf when you change.

The Bible is true, and the truth will set you free. Lewis has been won over by my behavior. How? Because "no corrupt communication proceed[ed] out of [my] mouth, but that which was good to the use of edifying, that it ministered grace" unto Lewis (Ephesians 4:29). All God wants us to do is lead by example—show people His love in our lives so they can be won over. So we need to stop looking at people, especially our spouses, through our eyes and start seeing them as God sees them.

When I wasn't doing what I should have been doing, I believe I stopped Lewis' spiritual growth. My witness of Christ was ugly. It had no love in it. My nagging, complaining, yelling, condemning, and talking back, then crying before the Lord, "Lord, I honor You," was hypocritical because we can't honor God when we don't honor the spouse He has given us. Also, the responsibility for doing right lies on the strongest individual in Christ. In my marriage, that was me. My responsibility was to continue developing my relationship with God. As I grew in the Lord by obeying His Word and letting Him work with Lewis, Lewis' relationship grew with God.

And men, your wife's failure to submit is not your excuse to disobey God. As the head of the household, you need to continue to lead by example and pray for her. The Bible says we can have whatsoever we say (Mark 11:24). Therefore, pray for what you want in your spouse with the Word of God. Although Lewis wasn't what I wanted him to be, every time someone at church asked about him, I would say, "He's fine. He is a man after God's own heart. He will do great works for Victory, and he will help finance the growth of our church." Guess what? I now have what I said.

What if you are married to a foolish person, as Abigail was in 1 Samuel 25? Her husband, Nabal, was a rich man, but he was "evil in his doings," stubborn and ill-mannered (v. 3). The Bible says Abigail was a woman of "good understanding" and "beautiful." Abigail was also a wise woman. David and his men protected Nabal's flocks and shepherds, but when David asked him for help, he refused and pretty much told them where to go. David was furious and decided to kill Nabal and his men. When Abigail was told that David was sending men to harm them and why, she immediately prepared a feast for David, treating him with the respect he deserved. She interceded for her husband. She knew the Word of God and told David that if he would not take revenge, God would reward him and take care of him. And that's just what happened.

This story is for both men and women. Just because your spouse may act foolishly, it doesn't mean that you should as well. Humble yourself before God and before your spouse. Use the wisdom God has given you. Pray that your spouse may have the wisdom of God if he or she is not yet who God would have him or her to be.

You Reap What You Sow

Love is not just a feeling. It is a deep, enduring concern for another's welfare. Marriage is hard for some and not for others. Why? Maybe because some went into it with a heart of giving and pleasing, while others went into it with selfishness and ungodly motives (for example, money, fame, loneliness, or running away from something). Marriage, contrary to popular opinion, is not give and take. It is not 50/50. It is what you can do for the other. It is all about giving. If you give, give, and give some more, after a while, the other person is going to want to bless you, so they give, give, and give in return. If both are giving, both are happy. Luke 6:38 says,

> For if you give, you will get! Your gift [love, respect, honor, money, peace] will return to you in full and overflowing measure, pressed down, shaken together to make room for more, and running over. Whatever measure you use to give—large or small—will be used to measure what is given back to you. (TLB)

This principle works negatively too. If you give criticism, anger, hatred, or lying, it will be given to you in greater measure. In Galatians, Paul echoes this truth: "Be not deceived, God is not mocked, for whatever a man soweth, that also shall he reap" (Galatians 6:7). Just remember: although you may think you give all the time, continue to give, for God is the rewarder. "He who plants and he who waters are equal [one in aim, of the same importance and esteem], yet each shall receive his own reward [wages], according to his own labor" (1 Corinthians 3:8 AB).

Putting It All Together

To sum up, what's wrong with our marriages? Why are they so messed up? Primarily because of three things:

- false expectations, unrealistic thoughts, preconceived ideas
- not realizing how we should live, according to God's Word
- selfishness, not having killed the flesh

What do you need to do to change your situation?

- Ask the Lord what He expects of you, and put your expectation in Him, not your spouse.

- You started with this book, but there is still so much more in the Bible! So read the Word and *do it*.
- Marriage is totally about giving, so give love, joy, peace, patience, kindness, goodness, faithfulness, gentleness, and self-control (Galatians 5:22-23).

I believe that any time you can see the Word, hear the Word, and understand the Word of God, you can be changed into that Word you see, hear, and understand. Once you are changed, God can use your marriage to His glory. "I know the thoughts that I think toward you, saith the Lord. Thoughts of peace, and not of evil, to give you an expected end" (Jeremiah 29:11). When they had no wine at the marriage ceremony, Jesus' mother had to awaken Him to the fact that it was time to do God's will for His life.

He said to her, "Woman, what have I to do with thee? Mine hour is not yet come."

She told the servants, "Whatsoever He says unto you, do it!"

No more excuses, whatever God tells you to do, *do it!* Pray this passage from Colossians 1:9-12 for your spouse:

> *For this reason, since the day You sent _____ to me, I have not stopped praying for _____ and our marriage and asking You to fill us with the knowledge of Your will through all spiritual wisdom and understanding.*

And I pray this is in order that
_____ *and I may live a life*
worthy of You, Lord, and may please
You in every way: bearing fruit in every
good work, growing in the knowledge of
God, being strengthened with all power
according to Your glorious might so
that we may have great endurance and
patience, and joyfully giving thanks to
the Father, who has qualified us to
share in the inheritance of the saints in
the kingdom of light. (My paraphrase of
the NIV)

Chapter 8
Happily Ever After

But all things are from God, Who through Jesus Christ reconciled us to Himself [received us into favor, brought us into harmony with Himself] and gave to us the ministry of reconciliation [that by word and deed we might aim to bring others into harmony with Him]. (2 Corinthians 5:18 AB)

The story of Sleeping Beauty says she and her prince lived happily ever. This walk with God is all about glorifying Him and bringing others to Christ. As Christians, we know that we are guaranteed a "happily ever after" because we are promised eternal life. Although there are no marriages in the resurrection, God wants us to live a happy, peaceful, and prosperous life in this marriage covenant, right now.

Be Like Christ

In Mark 16:15, Jesus told His disciples, "Go ye into all the world, and preach the gospel to every creature." Does this apply to those eleven disciples only? No. Does it pertain only to pastors? No. They couldn't possibly reach every creature. Instead, when we gave our lives to God, we chose to follow Christ, which makes us the disciples He continues to speak to and through.

Christianity is not a title. It is God using people on earth to be good witnesses for Christ. This walk of faith is not about you, your spouse, or even your children. It is about advancing the kingdom of God through every aspect of life. Unbelievers need to see Christ in us to want to become Christians.

In James 1:22-23, God says, "But be doers of the Word, and not hearers only, deceiving your own selves. For if anyone is a hearer only and not a doer, he is like a man holding a mirror seeing his natural face in a glass." That is why we need to do what the Word of God tells us because God is looking to see Himself in us. Remember, we are made in His image and likeness. God also wants us to see who we are in Christ. But if we don't do His Word, we don't become like Him. We are to exercise ourselves rather unto godliness (having God-like characteristics). When we accept Jesus and are led by the Spirit of God, we become children of God (Romans 8:14). Just as we reflect the physical and emotional characteristics of our earthly parents, so now we become transformed spiritually to reflect the personality of our Heavenly Father. For example, as a child I was raised by my stepfather and biological mother, so I have taken on the characteristics of my stepfather more than those of my biological father. Not to take anything away from my biological father, but my stepfather has had the greater influence on me. On the outside, I look just like my biological father, but the inside of me has characteristics of my stepfather. That is how, although we have an earthly father, we can still develop the characteristics and personality of our Heavenly Father. To do this, we must get to know Him on a very personal level by reading His Word and doing what He says. God is yearning to develop a relationship with you. I believe He said, "Finally, Jewell, I've been waiting to get to know you. I have so much for you to do, and I have so much to give to you."

As Paul tells us in 1 Corinthians:

> He that is joined unto the Lord is one spirit. . . . Know ye not that your body is the temple of the Holy Ghost who is in you, whom ye have of God, and ye are not your own? For ye are bought with a price; therefore, glorify God in your body and in your spirit, which are God's (6:17, 19-20).

In John 17:18, Jesus says, "As Thou hast sent me into the world, even so have I also sent them into the world." Just as God has sent Jesus into the world to preach the gospel, so God uses each of us and our marriages to preach the gospel. As Jesus is, so are we in this world (1 John 4:17).

Winning Souls

The story of Queen Vashti's refusal to come at the king's command, and the king's hasty decision to divorce her, has a lot to teach us. Remember, he was angry and asked his counselors what to do. He later realized that it was a mistake. He hadn't thought it through himself, and the men he turned to gave him self-serving advice. So here's a lesson for us: First take your problem to God; then choose wisely the people you'll talk to, because not everyone will give you good, godly advice. In the king's case, after he sobered up, he missed her. His counselors' advice took both the king and Vashti out of their destiny, and they sinned against God because they divorced. But God is good! He used that mistake for His glory by using Queen Esther to help the Jews.

Know that all Christians and non-Christians look at our marriages to see our standard of living. To the world, we are a live commercial for Jesus. If we divorce, it tells people that the Word doesn't work and there is no Jesus. When Lewis and I separated, my brother, who knows who I am in Christ, told me that he thought if any marriage would have succeeded, it would have been ours. He hoped my marriage was the one that would break the generational curse of divorce in our family.

As Christians, our marriages are looked on as examples to those outside in the world. Our marriages are a witness—it is not what we say; it's what we do and how we minister to other people. Our marriages are a window into God's love. No matter where you go, if people see God through you, they will seek you out for encouragement and spiritual advice. As Christians, we are to lead people to Christ or help those who have fallen get back to Him.

Second Corinthians 3:3 says we are living letters for Christ:

> You show that you are a letter from Christ, the result of our ministry, written not with ink but with the Spirit of the living God, not on tablets of stone but on tablets of human hearts. (NIV)

When my brother told me of his disappointment, I was hurt and sad because, ultimately, I was being a bad witness for Christ. God was not being glorified in my life, and I was just like others who didn't know Him. As Christians, we are not supposed to be like others in the world; we are supposed to be like Christ, and people should see that difference. Why would my brother want to get back with his wife if I couldn't keep my own marriage together? Although He still loves us, God gets upset when we don't fulfill our promises to Him and when we are bad witnesses. Why would people want to come to Christ if we are just like them? I was so ashamed, more so because my brother was not the only one watching. My separation stopped or slowed many family members and friends from accepting Jesus as Lord of their lives. It's not that the Word doesn't work. It is we who are not working the Word. Now, by the grace of God, Lewis and I have put our marriage back together and we are a living testimony that God's Word works if you do what it says.

Reconciliation

If your marriage is going through strife (dispute between two parties), you are not in harmony with your mate. You are going in opposite directions. Just as Christ died for you to be reconciled to God, you need to kill your flesh in order to be reconciled to your spouse.

For example, at the end of the month, you look at your bank statement against your check register. If they are not in agreement (harmony), you notify the bank and/or make the necessary changes to correct the problem. In a marriage, when you and your spouse are out of harmony, think of the Word of God as the bank statement you refer to during trials and tribulations. God's Word will reconcile you to your spouse.

As Christians, divorce is not supposed to be an option. However, there are two allowances in the Word of God for divorce: adultery and when nonbelievers want out. For women or men who are in an abusive situation, you may separate until your spouse gets help. However, remember that God's Word says, if you separate, you must remain single or be reconciled to your mate.

Husbands must understand the role and the responsibility they have toward God's daughters. God says in His Word, "Husbands in the same way be considerate as you live with your wives, and treat them with respect as the weaker partner and as heirs with you of the gracious gift of life, so that nothing will hinder your prayers" (1 Peter 3:7 NIV). That is serious. Can you imagine needing something from the Lord and not being able to go to Him in prayer because you haven't been treating your wife right? I am not talking about just violence. How do you talk to your wife? Do you treat her as the King's daughter that she is?

If even abuse, adultery, and homosexuality occur, know that God can still work in those situations. After all, the prophet Hosea married a prostitute. While married, she continued in that line of work and had two children who were possibly fathered by other men. However, Hosea continued to do what God had called him to do, and he and his wife reconciled.

If you are contemplating divorce or separation right now, *don't do it*. "For I consider that the sufferings of this present time [this present life] are not worth being compared with the glory that is about to be revealed to us and in us and for us and conferred on us!" (Romans 8:18 AB).

The Good Life

But as it is written, "Eye hath not seen, nor ear heard, neither have entered into the heart of man, the things which God hath prepared for them that love him" (1 Corinthians 2:9). God has a plan and a purpose for you and your spouse. I just recently discovered God's purpose for Lewis and me, and if I had divorced him, I would have destroyed God's plan and His call on our lives. You may say to yourself, "We are just average people who love the Lord." You may not see any gift that God can use in your marriage, but God says that He can use the foolish to put the wise to shame; the weak to put the strong to shame; and what is lowborn and insignificant to bring those in power to nothing. Why does He do that? So that we won't glorify ourselves but rather give Him the glory (1 Corinthians 1:26-31).

As with any other ministry, you have to be diligent, consistent, and work at it to glorify God. So right now,

1. Repent.
2. Turn your spouse over to God.
3. Forgive and forget as God does.
4. Renew your mind.
5. Be led by the Holy Spirit and not your flesh (die daily).
6. Establish a deeper relationship with your Heavenly Father.
7. Ask God what you should do to change and grow.
8. Be happy, and tap into His grace.

Heavenly Father, I can do nothing without You; but with You, I can do all things. I pray that You would open my spiritual eyes, my spiritual ears, prepare my heart, and renew a right spirit in me to hear from You daily. You have created this institution of marriage. Therefore, let my marriage forever glorify You. Let it be a testimony to others that You are true to Your Word and that Your way is perfect. Thank you for my man (or woman) of God. Thank you that the impartation of Your Word will change me first and that Your works through me may minister to my spouse. I give myself and my life's partner to You as Your own handiwork to do as You please. In Jesus' name, Amen, Amen, Amen.

About the Author

Jewell Powell was born in Atlantic City, New Jersey. When she was four years old, her mother and father moved to Maryland. Jewell met her husband, Lewis, in July of 1992, and she married her man of God in May 1996. They are the proud parents of two beautiful girls, Lauren and Diamond Powell. The Powell family resides right outside the Washington, D.C., metropolitan area.

Jewell earned a B.S. in Business and a M.S. in Contracts Management and has worked for the last 15 years in the contracts division at the U.S. Postal Service. She answered the call of God upon her life to write books after victoriously turning her marriage around by the power of God when it was headed to divorce court in 2001. After answering the call of God to write, she recognizes that it was only God who enabled her to do what she could never do on her own. Jewell's motto is, "But by the grace of God I am what I am: and his grace which was bestowed upon me was not in vain; but I laboured more abundantly than they all: yet not I, but the grace of God which was with me" (1 Corinthians 15:10).

Jewel accepted the Lord Jesus Christ in 1980. She and her husband are members of Victory Christian Ministry International, a Bible teaching church under the pastoral care of Tony and Cynthia Brazelton. She is an active participant in bringing God's vision to pass in the earth through the local body that God has called her to and has just completed the ministry's Ministerial Training School.